Introduction to Mental Health Billing

By Alice Scott
& Michele Redmond

Copyright January 2016

Disclaimer

Table of Contents

Billing for Mental Health Services
Introduction

Many of the people who enter the world of behavioral health go into private practice. In order to make sure they are properly reimbursed for their services they need to become familiar with billing health insurance companies or find someone they trust who can navigate this maze. Even if they find someone to handle it for them, it is wise to understand how everything works to make sure they get proper reimbursement for their services.

Most patients who have health insurance are covered for mental health benefits and they usually prefer to have the insurance pay for these services rather than pay themselves. In order to get the payment from the patient's insurance carrier, there are certain things that must be done within a set time frame and in a specific format.

Many things can affect the payment of a medical insurance claim. Participation with the insurance company, coding, forms, authorization, referrals, deductibles, coinsurance, and copays are just a few of the examples that can affect payments. Someone needs to be able to understand all this information and then act in such a way that is best suited to that situation. It can be a huge burden on the counselor, social worker, psychologist, or psychiatrist if they don't have someone to take care of these things for them.

The mental health provider who understands good business practices will be grateful to find someone skilled at submitting and tracking their claims. Whether they hire an employee or outsource to a billing service, the capabilities and experience of that person can make a tremendous difference in their income. If the person submitting the claims does not know how to handle both submitting the claims properly and making sure the claims are paid properly much of the income of the provider can be lost.

For a new mental health provider entering the field it can be difficult to understand why you don't just tell the insurance company how much they owe you and then they pay you. It doesn't work that way. Billing insurance companies and tracking correct payment of the claims is a very time consuming job. Often calls or letters to the insurance carriers are necessary to get claims paid. If not done correctly much income will be lost to unpaid, denied, lost or incorrectly paid insurance claims.

Insurance claims must be filed in a specific format within a certain "timely filing" period and in some cases must be filed electronically. Secondary and tertiary claims must be filed with copies of the primary (and secondary for tertiary claims) insurance payment. Claims are sometimes denied in error and must be challenged or appealed. Some claims are lost and never responded to. Checks are sometimes lost and never cashed. Claims are sometimes paid to the patient instead of the doctor.

To collect all the money that is due to a mental health provider, he or she needs to make sure a competent person is watching over all these potential problems and dealing with them in an effective efficient way. If they choose to hire someone and do the billing in house, they will need to have a good system in place to track all claims, insurance payments and patient payments. The best way to do this is with a practice management system which we go over in a later chapter.

Today most people have some form of health insurance that pays for part or all of the expenses of going to a doctor. There are many different kinds of health insurance policies and the services that are covered and the amount that is paid to the doctor vary depending on the policy.

Many people have health insurance offered thru their employment. Some are eligible for Medicare because of their age or due to a disability. Some no or low income people are eligible for their state Medicaid program. Others who work but may not have an option for health insurance such as the self-employed or those working in a small business are eligible for a low cost state sponsored program. These programs are usually based on income.

With the passing of the ACA, or Affordable Care Act in 2010, qualified individuals can purchase health care through their State Exchange. The problem with most of these plans is that the patient's out of pocket costs are very high. It is not uncommon for a patient to have a deductible of over $2000. In any case, most patients have some form of insurance.

Most insurance policies require that the patient pay a certain portion of the cost of the visit. The patient portion may be in the form of a deductible, a copay, or a coinsurance. Some do however cover services in full, or at 100%.

The patient may be required to pay different amounts depending on which provider he or she goes to. This amount may vary based on whether or not the doctor participates with the patient's insurance plan or what type of service they receive.

For example, a visit to a PCP (primary care physician) may require a $10 copay but a visit to a specialist may be a $25 copay. If a patient visits a participating provider they may only have a $10 copay, but if they go to a non-participating provider they may have a $200 deductible.

Not everyone is covered by health insurance. The ones that aren't covered are considered self-pay and just like in the old days these people must pay for their visits themselves. Some providers offer discounts or sliding scale fee schedules based on income to patients without health insurance.

When a patient does have health insurance, the bill for services must be submitted to the insurance carrier for payment and it is referred to as a claim. Claims can be submitted to the insurance carriers electronically or on paper. When submitted electronically, all of the required information is submitted in a specific format as required by the insurance carrier via internet connection.

When submitted on paper, the proper most up to date form must be used with all required information in the appropriate boxes and lines on the form. Once a claim is received by the insurance carrier it is reviewed to be paid, denied, or pended for further action. Of course the insurance carrier can deny ever receiving the claim and then it must be resubmitted.

Electronic submissions cut down on this since reports are sent out verifying receipt of the claim, but 15% of paper claims are mysteriously never received. We've even had carriers tell us they didn't receive a claim that was mailed in the same envelope with another claim that they did receive!

Some people have more than one insurance policy. When this is the case, the primary carrier must be billed first and then balance is billed to the second insurance carrier with the primary insurance payment information. If there is a third or tertiary insurance, it is billed last with payment information from the first two policies.

The insurance carriers have rules to determine which policy is primary or "prime" and which is secondary. The patient cannot choose which policy they want you to bill. We will cover this in more detail later.

In 2007 all healthcare providers were required to obtain an NPI number or National Provider Identifier. These NPI numbers are required in order to bill insurance claims or to refer a patient to another provider. So any provider who plans on billing insurance carriers or referring patients to other providers must obtain an NPI number.

These are all parts of medical billing that must be understood to do a good job at the process of bringing in the providers money and keeping the cash flow steady.

It is also important to know how it works so you do not inadvertently do anything illegal. When a provider participates with an insurance company, the provider must sign a legal contract agreeing to rules the person doing the billing must know. A mistake can be very costly and may even be construed as insurance fraud.

This book will go over all these parts and more of insurance billing so the reader obtains a good solid overview of the process.

Who Are Mental Health Professionals

There are many different types of mental health providers who specialize in many different areas. Some of the different credentials are:

Addiction counselors
Art therapists
Marriage and family therapists
Mental health counselor
Psychiatric nurse
Psychiatrist
Psychoanalyst
Psychologist
Psychotherapist
Religious counselor
Sex therapist
Social worker

Not all of these specialties are covered by medical insurance. Most commonly medical insurance covers services furnished by psychiatrists, psychologists, social workers, psychoanalysts, and in some cases a few others.

Psychiatrists are trained in the assessment, diagnosis, treatment and prevention of mental illness. They attend medical school and receive a M.D. and then receive additional training in their specific area of interest. Psychiatrists can provide counseling sessions, but many spend most of their time prescribing and managing medications. It is common for a patient to be seeing a psychiatrist and a psychologist or social worker at the same time.

Psychologists receive a degree of Psy.D. or Ph.D. and receive undergraduate training, licensing and certification. They treat a variety of conditions and some do psychological testing. In Louisiana and New Mexico specially trained psychologists can also prescribe medications.

Psychoanalyst is a general term covering many mental health providers. Psychoanalysts often have undergone extensive training and can be psychologists, social workers, or medical doctors. Psychoanalysis refers to the treatment of unconscious factors that may influence one's behavior and relationships. Often the treatment can go on for 5 to 10 years.

Psychiatric Nurses are licensed registered nurses with extra training in mental health. The services they can offer are determined by their level of training and experience. Under an MD's supervision they can treat help manage medications. In some states a psychiatric nurse is allowed to prescribe medications.

Psychotherapists are made up of a wide variety of mental health professionals. They provide counseling which can be more involved as it focuses on the patient's past along with feelings and experiences that tend to define the patient. It generally consists of regular sessions and extends from six months to two years.

Social Workers help people overcome social and health problems. Licensed clinical social workers (LCSW) cannot prescribe medications or order medical tests but they do provide therapy. Social workers may work in private practice or as case managers coordinating mental health with medical and other services such as in a hospital setting. MSWs or those social workers with a master's degree in social work cannot enroll with Medicare to treat Medicare patients. LCSWs can enroll in Medicare.

Marriage and family therapists evaluate patients with marriage or family relationship problems. Not all states require licensing or certification, but some insurance carriers do for joining their network. Medicare does not allow marriage or family therapists to enroll in Medicare. Therapy for marriage counseling averages 12 visits. These therapists also treat a variety of problems such as anxiety, depression, family conflict and eating disorders. Some insurance carriers will not pay for marriage counseling.

Addiction counselors usually have a degree in counseling, social work, or psychology and have special training in alcohol, drug, gambling and other addictions. They often treat their patients in group settings. Some insurance policies do not cover drug or alcohol treatment so benefits should definitely be verified. Generally addiction counselors are working at a facility rather than in private which often requires UB04 billing. The UB04 is a medical claim form similar to the CMS 1500 except it is for facilities such as hospitals, laser surgery centers, clinics, and rehab facilities. It requires the use of Rev codes, value codes, and type of bill. UB04 billing is a little more complicated than CMS 1500 billing.

Mental health counselor is a broad term for many providers who offer counseling. They treat a wide variety of problems from anxiety to depression and offer counseling for grief or stress. Whether or not insurance will cover claims will depend on the policy, the credentials of the provider and the enrollment status of the counselor. Licensed mental health counselors cannot enroll to treat Medicare patients.

Religious counselors are trained mental health counselors who also have extensive religious training. They provide counseling in a spiritual context. Religious counselors treat family and couples for problems, do group therapy, spiritual direction, and treat mental illness. Religious counselors are credentialed the same as other counselors so generally speaking insurance coverage is the same for seeking the help of religious counselors as it is for others.

Art therapy involves expressing yourself through various types of art to get in touch with hidden thoughts and feelings. It can help with mood disorders, depression, addiction and traumatic experiences. Art therapy is currently not covered by medical insurance.

How Participation with Insurance Carriers Affects the Billing

Many new providers do not understand the benefits of participating with insurance carriers. Whether or not a provider participates (or joins the panel) can affect not only how much the provider is paid, but can also affect his or her patient load. A mental health provider who pars with insurance companies will most likely build his or her practice quicker.

The provider who doesn't par with the insurance companies has basically a "cash" practice." Some insurance companies will pay for services to their patients for providers who are not in network (or don't Par). Payments usually go directly to the patient who is expected to pay at the time of service. However some insurance companies do not have any benefits for out of network (or non-par providers). In this case the patient will not get reimbursed anything.

Generally speaking, patients tend to go to doctors and other providers who participate with their insurance carrier so they know exactly what they will have to pay out of pocket. This is usually a set amount that is a co-pay or coinsurance. When a patient has insurance, they generally want to go to a provider that accepts that insurance as opposed to having to pay for their services themselves. Usually the patient's out of pocket expenses are less when they go to an in network or participating provider.

When the provider participates, he or she must then bill the insurance carrier for the service and receive part or all of the payment from the insurance company. The provider is required to accept the amount that the insurance company designates as "allowable".

They must also abide by all the rules of that insurance carrier regarding how and when that claim is filed and how the patient is medically treated. Referrals, authorizations, or treatment plans may be required. Some providers feel that the insurance companies are unreasonable and make them jump through hoops, but in our experience it is just a matter of understanding what is required of you.

However there are some carriers that require so much and reimburse so little that it is just not worth the provider participating.

In most cases participating with insurances will help to build a practice up but in some cases it truly isn't worth it. You need to make sure you consider the whole picture when deciding or helping the provider to decide whether or not to participate.

Having good systems in place to deal with insurance will help keep things running smoothly. For example, if a patient calls to make an appointment the insurance information should be obtained over the phone. This way the provider can make sure that whatever is required by the insurance carrier prior to seeing the patient for the first time (authorization or referral) is done.

You might be asking yourself by now how this affects you and your insurance billing. When a social worker or a doctor doesn't par with a major insurance carrier in your area, it may greatly cut down on the number of patients that will come to that provider because they will be paying more out of pocket. The provider is not even required to bill the insurance company on these patients and they may be submitting their own claims unless they are covered by Medicare. Medicare requires that the provider submit the claim for the patient even if they are non par.

Some doctors who don't par will submit the claims for the patient as a courtesy. But since payment goes to the patient it is almost impossible to track them. The provider just basically submits the claims once and the patient is responsible for making sure they get reimbursed. The patient usually pays the provider at the time of service.

When a provider decides to participate with an insurance carrier, the contract the provider signs is a legally binding contract between the two of them. The provider is required to follow the rules of the insurance company. Generally speaking what the insurance companies ask for in their contract is not unreasonable. The beginning provider can probably build his practice much quicker if he does participate with the major insurance companies in his area.

Pros of Participating

✓ Participating providers are listed in patient handbooks distributed by the insurance carrier to all the patients who are covered by the insurance
✓ Knowing exactly what the insurance carrier will pay the provider and approximately how long it will take them to collect the money
✓ Most patients look for providers who participate with their insurance
✓ Payment is made directly to the provider by the insurance carrier
✓ In many cases, payment to participating providers is higher
✓ Less likely for the patient to have a deductible to pay

Cons of Participating

✓   Insurance carriers determine the provider's fees

✓   Provider must wait for the payment from the insurance carrier (cannot collect at time of visit from patient)

✓   Provider must abide by the insurance company's rules

✓   Insurance carrier may require extra paperwork

✓   Provider may have to obtain or complete referral forms

✓   Provider may have to submit treatment notes or plans

✓   Provider must complete the credentialing application

✓   Provider must fit within the insurance company's guidelines

Pros of remaining Non Participating

✓   Provider can collect from the patient at the time of service

✓   Provider are not required to submit claims on your patient's behalf (many non par providers just provide the patient with a statement that they can submit on their own)

✓   Provider don't have to follow all of the insurance carriers rules

Cons of being Non Participating

✓   Patients like to go to Participating Providers
✓   Provider are not listed in the Insurance Company Directory
✓   Sometimes the patient will not be reimbursed unless the provider agrees to file treatment plans, or other info (so you end up doing paperwork anyway)
✓   Some plans have no out-of-network benefits so the patients will not be reimbursed anything
✓   Payment usually goes directly to the patient (if money is not collected up front, this can be a problem)
✓   Patients may have high out of network deductibles
✓   The provider must file claims to Medicare even if he or she does not participate and he or she must accept the limiting charge

Overall, for most providers it is beneficial to participate with most insurance plans. There are a few companies that are just more headaches for the provider than it is worth. You need to consider the provider's specialty, his patient base, and each individual carrier's requirements and reimbursement rate when making the decision.

There are actually a few insurance plans that reimburse better when a provider is out of network. It is rare but it does happen. So make sure you do your research with each company. You can request fee schedules from some companies. Medicare's fee schedule is posted on their website. This can be very helpful to the provider in making their decisions.

If the provider decides to participate with an insurance carrier it is a good idea for them to make sure they either read or at least fully understand everything that is in the contract before signing it. For example, most insurance carrier's contracts specify that the provider MUST collect the co-pay on plans where there is a co-pay. That means that the provider cannot just decide to waive the co-pay for patients and accept the insurance payment as payment in full.

Many providers will do this for some or all of their patients. For example, the patient is a friend or a neighbor or a relative and they are uncomfortable charging them the co-pay. Well, not charging them the co-pay is against the contract and if reported can cause the provider to be terminated from the insurance carrier. This requirement can actually work to the advantage of the provider. The provider can tell the patient that they must collect the co-pay or they can lose their participation status with the insurance carrier. That takes the problem of patients asking the provider to waive the co-pay out of the provider's hands.

Another common clause in many contracts is that the provider agrees to submit all claims timely. If the claim is not submitted timely and the claim is denied for timely filing, the provider cannot charge the patient, even the co-pay. Most providers know that they cannot charge the patient if the claim is denied, but they don't usually realize that keeping the co-pay is also breaking the contract.

Some providers don't realize that they cannot bill the patient and they do try to collect from the patient if the claim is denied. If the provider's office or billing service did not submit the claim in a timely manner then the patient is not liable. If the provider tries to collect and the patient reports it, the insurance carrier will investigate. They can decide to terminate the provider's contract if they feel that the provider has violated the terms.

Authorizations and Referrals

Some insurance policies require either authorizations or referrals. It is important to understand the difference between them. Referrals are obtained from the patient's PCP, or primary care physician. Authorization is obtained directly from the patient's insurance carrier.

Different insurance plans require different things. Some will not require any auth or referral. The provider needs to make sure he or she knows if a patient's insurance requires a referral or an authorization. A call should be made prior to seeing the patient. If this doesn't happen a claim may be denied for either no referral or no authorization. If a provider participates and an authorization or referral is required but not obtained the patient cannot be billed.

HMOs or Health Maintenance Organizations usually require that a patient have a PCP for their primary doctor. If the patient needs to see any other provider for any reason, usually a referral from their PCP is required. The provider they are referred to must also be in network with the HMO.

Many patients and providers found this to be too constrictive so insurance carriers came up with PPOs or Participating Provider Organizations. With a PPO a patient isn't required to have a PCP. If they choose to go to a participating provider they only have to pay a copay. If they choose to go out of network then they have a deductible and coinsurance. With PPOs authorization is required for certain services. PPO plans don't usually require referrals.

After several years of HMOs & PPOs insurance carriers decided to take the strengths from both types of plans and create yet another—EPO. EPOs are like HMOs in that you need to see a provider who is in network for the services to be covered by the insurance policy. However, like PPOs you don't need a referral from your PCP. Again certain services still require authorization. EPOs usually do not have any out of network benefits.

If an authorization is required it can usually be obtained by calling the insurance company and requesting it over the phone. Some companies have special forms that they want faxed in to them. Usually they will issue you a number or an alpha numeric reference number which you will enter on the insurance claim in box 23. If auths or referrals are something the provider runs into often it is important that they are dealt with properly to prevent denials.

Authorizations for mental health are usually given for a certain number of visits over a certain period of time. For example, you may be granted 6 visits from January 1st to May 31[st.] If the patient's treatment requires additional visits then the provider must request authorization for the additional visits. It is a good idea to request this auth prior to seeing the patient for more visits than the original authorization allowed. There is no guarantee that they will approve your request so you want to make sure you get the authorization prior to treating the patient.

Many times insurance carriers require forms called OTR's or outpatient treatment reports from the provider who is requesting the authorization for treatment. The OTR's usually need to be completed by the provider themselves as there are specific treatment related questions such as the goals of treatment, the objective measures, the progress, etc.

It is important to understand how much the authorization affects the payment and be able to keep track of when authorizations will run out, and what needs to be done to request more. Most practice management systems allow tracking the authorizations and will pop up warnings when the auth is going to expire, or if the patient is reaching the number of visits in the current authorization.

If a referral is required usually the patient has to obtain it from the primary care physician. The PCP must determine that the patient requires mental health services and complete a referral form for the insurance company. A copy of the referral is sent to the provider and a copy goes directly to the insurance company.

Referrals are usually only required once at the beginning of treatment. Patients are supposed to know their insurance plans and what is required by their insurance carriers. Some patients do and some patients don't. If the provider is par with their insurance plan then it is also their responsibility to understand the requirements as well. Bottom line, if you want to ensure payment you should make sure all requirements are met.

If you find out after services were rendered that an auth or referral was required but not obtained you can see if the insurance carrier will backdate one to the initial date of service. This is called a retroactive auth or referral. Many companies will only backdate an auth or referral few days if at all. Some won't backdate at all.

If services were somehow provided without the required auth or referral you should try to obtain one after the fact. If there were any extenuating circumstances as to why an auth or referral was not obtained, an appeal can be filed. A large percentage of appealed claims are paid upon appeal.

For example, if a phone call was made prior to the initial visit but the customer service representative provided inaccurate information such as no auth is required when indeed it was, you should file an appeal. Make sure to include all information such as the name of the representative, the date and time of the call and the information that was given. There is no guarantee that they will grant it, but it is worth the effort.

Forms

Not many forms are required for mental health billing. An intake sheet, or patient demographic form, and signature form for the office HIPAA practices are about it. We've included a sample intake sheet. It is a good idea to get photocopies of the insurance cards to keep with the completed intake sheet for insurance billing purposes.

All medical offices are required to follow HIPAA laws. The office HIPAA policies and procedures should be made available to all patients. A copy does not have to be given to every patient, but it does have to be available to any patient upon request. It is a good idea to have each patient sign a statement saying that they were made aware that the office's HIPAA policy is available to them. It should be signed and dated, and it should be updated periodically. For example, you may want to have the patient sign the statement once a year.

Psychotherapy notes taken by the provider are protected under HIPAA laws and are separated from the rest of the patient's medical record. Notes taken by the provider cannot be disclosed except under extreme circumstances.

Sample HIPAA statement:

Janice Jones Ph. D. has made me aware that a copy of their HIPAA policies and procedures is available to me upon request.

_____

Signature of patient   Date Signed

On the patient demographics sheet, you will want to gather all the personal information on the patient that you may need, not only for billing purposes but for treating the patient as well. The obvious is the patient's name, address, date of birth, contact information such as phone numbers and/or email, and insurance information.

Mental health providers generally do not require a superbill for reporting services. Many mental health providers are seeing the same patients repeatedly over time for the same codes so they can report the billing information to the biller in a much simpler form than other medical specialties. Many of our mental health providers send us a list of names of patients they saw for usually a week's time frame. We need only the name of the patient and the date of service. Our practice management system has the patient demographics stored along with the diagnosis.

If there are any changes or they saw the patient for a different service, they can just indicate it. For example the provider may normally see the patient for 45 minutes and bill a 90834. The patient comes in and has a small crisis and the provider spends 60 minutes. They can just write that next to the patient's name so the billing goes out as a 90837.

When a new patient is seen by a mental health provider, a patient intake sheet is required to enter all the patient demographics. Once the biller has the demographics and knows the diagnosis, all that is required for future visits is the date of service unless the codes change.

If a provider is billing in-house then they will also need forms to submit insurances claims. Commercial insurances and no-faults are billed on CMS 1500 forms. They are the standard insurance claim form provided by CMS or the Centers for Medicare and Medicaid Services. Per HIPAA, all insurance claims must be submitted on these preprinted red and white CMS 1500 forms. The current version is the CMS 1500 (rev 02-12).

Providers also need to have patients sign statements indicating that they authorize the release of information regarding their treatment to their insurance company. They also need to sign a statement authorizing payment to be made directly to the provider. The following are examples are examples of these statements:

Release of Information

I authorize the release of any medical or other information necessary to process insurance claims.

_____.

Release of payment to provider

If you participate with the insurance company and want payment made directly to you get a signed release of payment statement such as this:

I authorize payment of medical benefits to the provider for services of these insurance claims. _____

Keep these forms in the patient's files. You are not required to have the patient sign a form each time they come in. Have them sign the form once and keep it on file.

Intake Sheet

Here is an example of an intake sheet you could use for information you require from the patient along with the necessary releases.

Patient Intake Sheet
Janice Smith PsyD
25 Mary Terrace
New Hartford, N Y 13413

Patient name _____ Insured_____

Date of Birth _____ Date of Birth _____

SS# _____ SS# _____

Address _____Address _____

_____   _____

Phone _____Relationship to patient _____

Marital Status S M D W   Other(circle)Marital Status S M D W Other

Employer _____ Employer_____

Primary Insurance _____
Address for claims _____

D # _____   Group # _____

Secondary Insurance info

_____

D# _____   Group # _____

Have you seen any other provider for this problem? _____yes   _____ no

Medicare

Some people who seek mental health services are covered by Medicare; either regular Medicare (Part B) or by a Medicare Advantage Plan (Part C). If they are covered by Medicare Part B their benefits for mental health services are paid at the regular Medicare benefits fee schedule and are subject to a yearly deductible. Once the deductible has been met, Medicare pays 80% of the allowed amount.

If the patient is covered by a Medicare Advantage Plan, the claims are processed by the insurance carrier of the plan they enrolled in. There are several choices that the patients have for Medicare Advantage Plans. Some of the more common ones are United Healthcare Medicare, Blue Cross Medicare and American Progressive Todays Options.

Patients have the option of keeping their regular Medicare benefits or enrolling into one of the many Medicare Advantage Plans. Even though the plans offer the same benefits as regular Medicare the benefits can vary greatly.

The benefit of choosing an advantage plan is that the patient's out of pocket expenses are usually less. Most advantage plans have a co-pay as opposed to the deductible and 20% co-insurance with regular Medicare Part B.

When a patient presents their insurance information and state they have Medicare it is important that it is verified whether they have regular Medicare or if they have enrolled in one of the Medicare Advantage Plans. The claims need to be submitted to the correct carrier. If you submit a claim to the Medicare Part B carrier and the patient is enrolled in a Medicare Advantage Plan, the services will be denied stating "claim not covered by this payer/contractor."

Regular Medicare requires electronic submissions of claims. Providers may apply for a waiver to file on paper. There are certain criteria that a provider must meet to be eligible for the waiver and an application must be completed or a letter must be sent to the Medicare contractor for the area that the provider is in. If the provider is not eligible for a waiver they must file all Medicare claims electronically.

Personally, I would strongly suggest submitting them electronically. Electronic submissions are easier to track and paid faster than paper claims. If you are using a practice management system it should be capable of submitting electronically. There are many clearing houses out there that submit to Medicare carriers. You just need to contact them to make sure they connect to the Medicare carrier that you need and see if they are compatible with your practice management system. Some clearinghouses are free of charge and some do charge fees. Make sure you look into their fees before enrolling.

If you do not have a practice management system that is capable of submitting claims electronically, Medicare has a free software available called PC-ACE. It is usually downloadable from their website. PC-ACE software will allow you to submit claims electronically to Medicare but it does not allow you to track the claims. It does not replace the practice management system.

If you are using a practice management system but are submitting Medicare claims with PC-ACE, you will have to double enter the claims. You will have to enter them into PC-ACE to submit them and then into your practice management system in order to track them.

Medicare fee schedules are available online at the Medicare carrier's website if you wish to know what Medicare allows for treatment. Simply go to the website and locate the fee schedule. The allowed amount for any procedure or service can be looked up by CPT code. Many providers will use the Medicare allowed amount to help them determine their fees. They sometimes take the allowed amount for a particular CPT code and multiply it by 130% - 150% and round it off to use for their regular fee. For example, if the Medicare allowed amount for CPT code 90834 is $85 then $85 times 150% would be $127.50. So the provider might want to make his fee for a 90834 $125 or $130.

In 2008 George Bush signed a mental health parity act designed to prevent restrictions by insurance carriers to limit benefits of patients and limit out of pocket expenses for the insured on psychotherapy charges. Many states put into effect their own mental health parity laws as well.

The federal act stated that mental health benefits must be equal to the benefits for medical treatment. Co-pays could not exceed co-pays charged for medical office visits. If a policy allowed for out of network benefits then mental health benefits must also be covered out of network. There could be no separate deductibles for mental health coverage.

This act did not cover everyone. Employers with 50 or less employees are exempt from this law. This also did not cover brief office visits to monitor or change prescriptions for medications.

Medicare has its own plan. They called it "elimination of discriminatory co-payment rates for Medicare outpatient psychiatry services".

Previously

From January 1, 2010 through December 31, 2011 Medicare covered 55% of the allowable rate. So the patient was responsible for 45% of the cost for any services rendered in 2010 and 2011. In 2012 Medicare covered 60% and in 2013 65%. So in 2012 the patient paid 40% and for 2013 the patient is responsible for 35%. Finally in 2014 Medicare will pay the full 80% it now covers for medical benefits while the patient will be responsible for 20%.

If a provider wants to treat Medicare patients they must enroll to become a Medicare Provider. They can enroll as a participating or non-participating provider. If they are participating, Medicare will make payments directly to the provider. If they are non-participating payment is made to the patient. Providers who are not enrolled in Medicare cannot treat Medicare patients.

PQRS

PQRS (Physician Quality Reporting System) is an extremely complicated system of reporting quality care to Medicare patients. Prior to 2015 PQRS was simply an incentive program know as PQRI (Physician Quality Reporting Initiative), an initiative which paid an incentive to providers for using the reporting system. But in 2015 it became a penalty program which is now going to penalize providers who do not use the system by applying payment adjustments to physicians who do not satisfactorily report the quality measures. Providers who do not report performance measures using PQRS will be faced with a 1.5% penalty in 2015 and a 2% penalty in 2016. The penalty for 2015 is based on reporting done in 2014. PQRS applies to most providers who bill services for Medicare patients.

CMS states that the first step is to determine if the provider is eligible to participate in PQRS. A list of PQRS eligible providers can be found at:
http://www.cms.gov/Medicare/Quality-Initiatives-Patient-Assessment-Instruments/PQRS/Downloads/PQRS_List-of-EligibleProfessionals_022813.pdf

The PQRS program is for Fee-For-Service Medicare patients. It does not include patients who are enrolled in Medicare Advantage Plans, or Part C Medicare.

There are four different methods for reporting PQRS. First, determine which reporting method best fits their practice. Here are four methods:

> Claims based
> Registry Reporting
> EHR Based Reporting
> Group Practice Reporting Option (GPRO)

Claims based reporting is the traditional reporting option. It involves submitting CPT-II or G Codes on the Medicare claims for the patients being reported. In order to qualify using the claims based option, an eligible provider must satisfactorily report on at least 50 percent of eligible instances. (We are going to cover the claims based reporting option and the G codes in depth in our next newsletter.)

Registry Reporting is done through qualified registries.   Qualified registries are vendors that submit quality measure data to CMS using a source other than an EHR. Providers would manually input or upload the patient data into the qualified registry. The qualified registry then calculates the PQRS and submits those calculations to CMS.

EHR Based Reporting is done through an Electronic Health Record system. Providers may submit PQRS measures through a qualified EHR system. The qualified EHR system vendor would forward that data on to CMS.

Group Practice Reporting Option is done when a group of providers opts to participate in PQRS as a group practice. The members of a group who opts into the Group Practice Reporting Option (GPRO) relinquish their right to participate in PQRS as an individual provider. The PQRS incentive is then calculated based on the group's total estimated Medicare Part B charges for the year.

Once the method is determined it is important to set up an office workflow to make sure the reporting is completed. If using the traditional reporting option, or claims based reporting, then the codes used to report PQRS could be added to the encounter form. If a paper encounter form is used then that would be fairly easy. The provider can simply check off the appropriate reporting codes and the biller would simply add them to the claim when it is billed. If the provider uses an electronic system then the codes need to be added to that system so that they can be reported on the claims. The important thing is to establish a system to ensure that the PQRS reporting is done.

Most mental health providers use the claims based reporting method. The following is a run down of how to report using the claims based method:

1.   Identify the measure you will use – CMS has over 300 reporting measures but (thankfully) most are not relevant for mental health. There are really only 9 measures that relate to mental health and they are:

1.   107 Adult Major Depressive Disorder: Suicide Risk Assessment
2.   128 Body Mass Index Screening and Follow-Up
3.   130 Documentation of Current Medications in Medical Record
4.   131 Pain Assessment and Follow-up
5.   134 Screening for Clinical Depression and Follow-up Plan
6.   181 Elder Maltreatment Screen and Follow-up Plan
7.   226 Tobacco Use: Screening and Cessation Intervention
8.   247 Substance Abuse Disorders (counseling regarding options)

9. 248 Substance Abuse Disorders (Screening for depression)

•   Remember, the performance measure must be reported using the appropriate g-code or CPT-II code, but the actual results do not get reported.

2. Link the chosen measure to the appropriate reporting code – Find the appropriate G-Code or CPT II code to report the measure. Make sure the procedure code that is being billed is appropriate for the measure being reported.

Click here to see a table showing the measures, or go to http://www.solutions-medical-billing.com/support-files/pqrstablementalhealth.pdf, the CPT codes and the reporting codes (info from CMS) (* Please note that this information is always changing. Please check the CMS website to make sure that you are using the most up to date codes. For example, this chart shows measure 106 which was deleted as of January 1, 2015.)

So now that we have covered the steps of PQRS, let's go through a couple of examples:

Psychologist Dr Jones sees a patient for the first time and diagnoses the patient as having Major Depressive Disorder. He performs an assessment of the severity of the Major Depressive Disorder during the initial visit. The claim for the initial visit could be coded as follows:

1. 09/04/2014   90791 $225.00
2. 09/04/2014   G8930 $ 0.00

LCSW Mary Smith sees a patient that she has been seeing fairly regularly for the past 12 months. The patient missed the past couple of scheduled appointments and Mary sees some changes in the patient so she decides to screen the patient for clinical depression. After completing the screening she determines that the patient is not clinically depressed. The patient was seen for a 45 minute session and may be coded as follows:

1.	09/04/2014	90834	$125.00
2.	09/04/2014	G8510	$ 0.00

Report the measures to Medicare – Measures can be reported to Medicare in one of four different ways:

1. Claims based reporting – codes are included on the claim for the services
2. Registry based reporting – measures are reported to large Medicare approved organizations that report the data to Medicare
3. EHR based reporting – measures are reported through the EHR system
4. Group practice reporting – measures are reported through a group practice

The most common reporting method is claims based reporting. Claims based reporting is done by adding a G-Code or a CPT II code to the claim. Once the appropriate code is selected it is billed on the same claim as the services. The code must be entered with either a $0.00 or a $0.01 charge. (Nothing is paid on the code. Some systems will not allow it to be entered with a $0.00 charge so a $0.01 charge must be used. It will depend upon the system being used to create the claim.) So now that you understand how the coding is done you need to understand what patients need to be reported. In order to avoid the penalty practitioners must report on at least 50% of eligible instances. Keep in mind this is only in regards to patients with traditional part B Medicare. Even though it is only required to report on 50% of eligible cases it is a good idea that practitioners routinely report on all Medicare part B patients even if they are simply reporting that no screening was done. That will ensure that they avoid the penalty. But simply reporting the codes is not enough. Practitioners must also make sure that their documentation reflects the PQRS code reported.

Many people feel that PQRS just puts added paperwork on the practitioner and their staff. It does take a little additional effort on behalf of the provider but some feel that it will act as a brief reminder to the provider to perform these essential tasks that they should be performing regularly. The reality is that if you take the time to figure out what needs to be done it really doesn't take that much extra effort to implement it. However, there are some providers who are just willing to take the penalty or will choose to no longer treat Medicare patients.

Providers do not need to notify CMS or their Medicare regional carrier prior to beginning reporting. Simply add the codes to the claims and submit. Many providers and billers are avoiding figuring out what PQRS is because it seems too complicated. But avoiding it will end up costing the provider money. How much money is lost will depend on how many Medicare patients the provider sees.

Medicaid

Medicaid is a state sponsored program for uninsured, low income people so it varies from state to state. Many states have Medicaid HMO's, or Medicaid Managed Care Plans, which are administered by individual insurance carriers. Patients who are eligible for Medicaid can usually choose which Medicaid Managed Care Plan they would like to have. Not all Medicaid providers are also providers for all Medicaid Managed Care Plans. Patients many times think that even if they have enrolled in a Medicaid Managed Care Plan that they have Medicaid and only present their Medicaid ID card to their providers. They don't understand the difference and that claims go to the managed care carrier.

To ensure payment for services it is important that the provider or provider's staff verifies the insurance. If the patient has a managed care plan that the provider is not in network with, the provider will not be paid and in many cases the patient cannot be billed.

In New York state social workers cannot bill for straight Medicaid. They can however see Medicaid HMO patients if they participate with that plan. The rules vary so much that you need to check into the state laws of the state that you are billing.

Since Medicaid is a state sponsored plan the rules of billing vary from state to state. If you will be billing Medicaid claims you should find the billing guidelines for the state you are billing. For example, New York State has special forms that must be used if submitting claims on paper. Other states require the CMS form. There may be other billing requirements. Most states have their billing guidelines available on their website. Many also offer seminars throughout the year.

Medicaid claims also can usually be submitted electronically as well. As with Medicare many clearinghouses are set up with Medicaid to submit claims. As long as the clearinghouse is compatible with the practice management system used, claims can be submitted electronically. Again, make sure to check into the fees that the clearinghouse will charge.

Medicaid offices in many states have the capability of allowing claims to be submitted through their websites. This is similar to using the free Medicare software, PC-ACE. If you are using a practice management system, the claims will still have to be entered into that as well as the online system.

Workers Comp, Auto and Personal Injury Claims

You may occasionally get a patient whose services are related to a work injury or auto accident and their claims must be filed to the workers compensation carrier or auto carrier. In order to make sure these services are covered it is a good idea to check with the individual insurance carrier to make sure they are authorizing payments.

Although it is not common for mental health providers to get many no fault or workers comp claims it does happen. For example, a person who works for a grocery store that was robbed may have post traumatic stress disorder from the ordeal. Or a person who was involved in a serious car accident that took the life of a loved one may have an adjustment disorder. Again, it is not common but it does happen. It is good to understand how to bill them if they come up.

Since these claims are not the same as health insurance claims, the patient will have not usually have an identifying ID card with ID number. In the case of auto accidents, get the claim number, the proper insurance carrier, phone number, and address. Auto accident claims can be filed on a CMS 1500 form.

A workers comp claim requires a workers comp case number and a carrier case number. Call the insurance carrier and make sure the services are authorized. There are different requirements as to what qualifications you must hold to counsel workers comp patients. For example, NYS does not allow LCSW's to treat workers comp patients unless supervised by a psychologist.

Some states will allow you to file claims on a CMS 1500 form, but some will require that you file on a special workers' comp form designed by the state. When you make your initial call to the insurance company to check to make your services will be covered ask on which form the insurance carrier would prefer that you submit your claims. The claims are filed using the same ICD10 and CPT codes that are used for commercial claims.

Commercial Insurance Carriers

Commercial insurance carriers all have different plans with different rules. Commercial insurance plans can be indemnity, PPO, EPO, or HMO plans. There is no way to explain each and every plan in detail. How they affect a provider also depends on if the provider is participating or in network. If a provider is participating then it will be much more important that they know each plan and their rules.

If a patient comes in with an insurance that you are not familiar with the best thing to do is call the number on the back of the card to verify the mental health benefits. Patients are not usually happy if they go to a provider thinking that their insurance is going to cover the visit and then end up being billed later on. It is best to find out up front if their insurance is going to cover the services or not.

Some insurance carriers use a third party administrator to handle their mental health benefits. For example, United Health Care uses United Behavioral Health (UBH) for some of their plans. That means that even though the patient has United Health Care and gives a copy of their United Health Care insurance card the claims actually go to United Behavioral Health. The provider must be par with United Behavioral Health if they wish to be in network.

Mental health benefits vary greatly from plan to plan. Some plans may require a referral from the patient's PCP. Others may require authorization for treatment. Still others may not require a referral or an authorization but they may limit the number of visits allowed per year. The best thing to do is to check a patient's benefits before they start treatment.

In the past, many insurance carriers used to discriminate against mental health services by having different benefits for mental health than for medical services. For example, a patient could have a plan that paid 80% of covered charges for any medical services, but they only paid a flat $10 for a mental health visit. The patient responsibility in some cases exceeded 80%. Over the years, lawmakers have passed many laws trying to even out the playing field.

One such law was the Mental Health Parity and Addiction Equity Act of 2008. MHPAEA is a federal law that provides participants who already have benefits under mental health and substance use disorder (MH/SUD) coverage parity with benefits limitations under their medical/surgical coverage. This stopped insurance carriers from having separate reimbursement rates for mental health services and basically said that the benefits for mental health services must be equal with the benefits for medical services.

Of course there are exceptions for these laws. For example, businesses with less than 50 employees, employers who do not currently offer mental health benefits, and individual insurance plans are all exempt from MHPAEA. That excludes a lot of people but they are trying to stop the discrimination.

Even with the new laws, it is not uncommon for a patient to have different benefits for mental health than they do for medical visits. For example, they may have a $15 co-pay for medical visits but they have a $25 co-pay for mental health visits. This information should also be obtained when calling to request benefits or some insurance carriers allow providers to look up benefit information online.

When calling to verify benefits you can use the following guidelines.

"Hi I am <your name> and I am calling from <office name> to verify outpatient mental health benefits for a <provider's credentials ie. LCSW, PhD, PsyD, MD>.

The representative will then look up the patient by ID# and ask for personal information such as address or social security number of the patient. You should have this information available when you make the call. The following information may be needed.

Effective date
Auth required
Referral required
Deductible
Co-pay
# of visits allowed
OTR required
Address for claims submission – not necessary if claims are being submitted electronically.

The following form may be copied and used to record benefit information on patients.

Patient's Name

_____DOB_____

Address _____SS# _____

_____

Insurance Carrier _____Phone_____

ID# _____Group# _____

Effective date _____

Auth required _____sometimes a different #
needs to be called_____

Referral required _____

Deductible ___yes ____ no $_____ amount _____If
deductible paid _____ how much _____

Copay _____ # of visits allowed _____

OTR required ___yes ____ no when required_____

Address for claims submission

_____

_____

Commercial insurance claims are filed on CMS 1500 forms unless they are submitted electronically. We go into submitting claims in detail later on.

CPT Codes

CPT Codes - or Current Procedural Terminology are services and codes that describe procedures performed by providers of health care services. These codes are used to report the services that were provided to the patient. CPT Codes are copyright material and owned by the AMA. We cannot list them individually with descriptions but below are the ranges that are used in billing mental health services. On January 1, 2013 there were significant changes to the CPT codes for mental health providers. The codes below reflect the codes effective January 1, 2013.

Daignostic or Evaluative Interview Procedures

90791 thru 90840 are evaluation or interview procedure codes for specific limits of time for outpatient services. CPT codes are updated yearly. Some new codes are added and some codes are deleted. Always use the most current CPT codes.

There used to be separate CPT codes that covered interactive psychotherapy for either 20 – 30 minute or 45 – 50 or 75 – 80 minutes of face to face psychotherapy and without medication management. Now the same CPT codes as mental health in the office are used, but there is also an add on code of 90785 to indicate interactive.

There used to be separate codes for inpatient hospital or residential care facility of face to face psychotherapy for specified periods of time and with and without medication management. Now the same CPT codes as mental health in the office are used. Just the place of service is different. Most insurance plans including Medicare do not cover psychotherapy services for patients who are in the hospital.

90845 – 90899 are other therapies including family therapy sessions, group sessions, and medication management with no therapy.

Telephone therapy sessions are becoming more and more common. There is not a specific CPT code for this service. It can be billed using the 90899 but most insurance carriers do not cover telephone sessions.

CPT codes also referred to as procedure codes are what providers use on claims to tell the insurance carrier what service or services the patient received. Providers should have a fee associated with each CPT code they use. For example, if a psychologist sees a patient for the first time and does a psychiatric diagnostic evaluation or a new patient evaluation, they would use CPT code 90791. If the psychologist charges $200 for a new patient visit, the fee for 90791 would be $200.

ICD9 Codes

Prior to October 1, 2015, ICD9 Codes were the diagnosis codes used to report the condition of the patient. ICD10 codes replaced the ICD9s. Any dates of service prior to 10/1/2015 must be coded with ICD9 codes. Services after October 1, 2015 must be coded using ICD10 codes. There are online sites to look up diagnosis codes as they are not copyright protected. This is a site we have used for many years to look up ICD9 codes.

http://www.icd9coding1.com/flashcode/home.jsp

If this site is not available, google 'free online icd9 codes'.

When choosing a diagnosis code, make sure you code it to the highest level of specificity. That means that if there is a fourth or fifth digit for the code that you are using, you must use it. For example, depression, code 311 has no fourth or fifth digits that apply, so you just use the 311. But simple type schizophrenia, 295.0, must have a fifth digit of 0-5 to describe the subcategory. So if you sent in a claim with diagnosis 295.0 it would be denied. You must have a fifth digit such as 0 and use code 295.00.

Very often when a claim is denied for a valid diagnosis code it is because it is truncated or not complete and requires another digit. The online site we recommended above makes it easy to determine whether another digit is required or not and lists the possible choices. Searches can be done numerically or alphabetically. For example, if you know that you are looking for a diagnosis for anxiety but you can't remember the 5th digit for anxiety with panic attack you can just enter 300. And it will list all anxiety diagnosis codes. Or you could enter "anxiety" and also get a list of all anxiety codes.

ICD10 Codes

The ICD10 Codes, or **International Statistical Classification of Diseases and Related Health Problems,** are the diagnosis codes. They are the specific descriptions of the disease or illness that the services are being performed for. The Department of Health and Human Services changed ICD9 codes to ICD10 codes effective October 1, 2015. ICD10 codes are an important part of the effort to develop nationwide electronic health records. ICD9 codes were limited to 17000 codes where ICD10 codes allow for 155,000 codes.

ICD9 codes were not just being expanded. ICD10 codes are totally different than ICD9 codes. It isn't a case of just add another number and there aren't just a few small changes. ICD10 codes identify much more information about the visit than ICD9s do. ICD10 codes contain an expansion of disease classification with greater specificity. They are much more detailed than ICD9s and will help identify fraudulent billing practices.

In addition to being updated regularly, ICD codes are also revised periodically. Prior to October 1, 2015 ICD9 codes were used to report diagnoses. In 1992 they developed the ICD-10 version which is used to tract mortality statistics. The ICD-11 version is expected to be released in the future and will utilize the Web 2.0 principles

ICD10 codes identify much more information on the patient's visit than an ICD9 code. ICD10 codes contain an expansion of disease classification with greater specificity. They will be much more detailed and will help identify fraudulent billing practices.

ICD10 coding requires more clinical information such as "did the patient use tobacco", "did the patient use alcohol", "which finger was cut", "which part of the finger", "was the nail damaged". The new codes contain alpha characters as well as numeric. The number 1 can mean 15 different things.

The AMA has some great resources on ICD 10:

http://www.ama-assn.org/ama/pub/physician-resources/solutions-managing-your-practice/coding-billing-insurance/hipaahealth-insurance-portability-accountability-act/transaction-code-set-standards/icd10-code-set.shtml

ICD10 codes are used to report the diagnosis or the reason for the patient's visit. There may be one diagnosis or multiple diagnoses. For example, a patient may be seen for depression and anxiety. The ICD10 code for depression is F32.9 and the ICD10 code for anxiety is F41.9. Both codes would be reported on the claim. On the CMS 1500 (rev 02-12) ICD10 codes are reported in box 21 fields a-1. There is room to report up to twelve diagnosis codes on a claim form.

Using Modifiers

Sometimes it is necessary to use modifiers on insurance claims. Modifiers are 2 digits that are used to further describe a service or procedure. There are not a lot of modifiers that pertain to mental health billing but there are a couple that in some cases are required to adequately describe the services to insure proper reimbursement by an insurance carrier.

Modifiers should never be added by a biller just to get a service paid. A modifier should only be added if it is needed to explain the services further than the cpt code. Only the provider or a coder who is reading the patient's notes can determine if a modifier is appropriate. If a biller suspects that a modifier might be appropriate, they should check with the provider.

Many times we are asked "what modifier can I add to xxxxx to get it paid?" It is fraudulent to add a modifier strictly to increase reimbursements. Modifiers must be used appropriately.

Modifiers go in box 24D on the CMS 1500 claim form, right after the CPT code. There is room for up to 4 modifiers. Usually only one is needed, but sometimes there is a need to use multiple modifiers. The following is a list of modifiers that maybe applicable for mental health services.

Modifiers are not as common with mental health as they are with other specialties, but they are still needed in certain situations. It is good to know what they stand for and how they should be used.

The GQ modifier is used when services are rendered via a synchronous telecommunications system.

The GW modifier is used when services rendered are unrelated to the patient's terminal condition. It is used when the patient is enrolled in Hospice but the services being billed are not related to the patient's terminal condition.

The GT modifier is used when services are rendered via interactive audio and video telecommunications system.

The HJ modifier is sometimes used to indicate EAP visits.

Nursing Home, Assisted Loving and Home Visits

Many times nursing homes will seek mental health providers that are willing to come into the nursing home and treat patients. This can be a good situation for a mental health provider. They don't need to market as the nursing home supplies the patients for them. They don't need to maintain office space unless they wish to see patients in an office setting in addition to the nursing home. There are a lot of pluses.

Nursing home visits are very similar to office visits. The provider just travels to the facility instead of the patient traveling to the office, and sees each patient either right in their room, or in an area provided by the facility. Providers can provide either psychotherapy or medication management visits. More information is available on billing medications later in "Medication Management."

Most nursing home patients have Medicare or a Medicare Advantage Replacement Plan. Medicare allows for mental health counseling in a nursing home setting. Medicare will not reimburse the mental health provider if they bill independently if the patient is in their first 100 days of their stay, or in the Medicare Part A portion of their stay. Medicare covers the nursing home fees for the patient's first 100 days of their stay and their fee is supposed to be all inclusive. If a patient needs mental health care in the first 100 days then it is the responsibility of the nursing facility to cover that cost.

If you are a mental health provider, or you bill for a mental health provider who treats nursing home patients, it is important to verify if the patient is in their first 100 days prior to treatment. It can be difficult to get reimbursement from the facility if a patient is mistakenly seen during that time.

CPT codes for nursing home patients are now the same as the CPT codes for regular office visits. In the past there were different CPT codes for nursing home visits but now the cpt codes are the same as if the patient was seen in the office but the place of service code changes. Place of service codes for nursing facilities are as follows:

31 - Skilled Nursing Facility
32 - Nursing Facility
33 - Custodial Care Facility

The place of service code depends on the type of bed the patient is in. That information must be provided to you by the nursing facility. If a provider sees a patient (or patients) in a nursing facility then the facility will usually provide a face sheet for the patient showing all of the demographics including insurance information.

Patients can also be seen in their homes or in assisted living facilities. The same CPT codes and ICD10 codes are used to report these visits. Only the place of service code changes. Most insurances including Medicare cover mental health service in both of these locations. The Place of service codes are:

12 - Home
13 - Assisted Living Facility

Medication Management

Some mental health illnesses require treatment with medications which may be prescribed by a psychiatrist. As of this writing there are two states, New Mexico and Louisiana who also license psychologists after very specific training to treat mental illness with medication after consulting with a psychiatrist. There are also a very few psychologists who are authorized by the Dept of Defense to treat mental illness with prescription medications.

Psychiatrists are trained in the assessment, diagnosis, treatment and prevention of mental illness. They attend medical school and receive an M.D. and then receive additional training in their specific area of interest.

Psychiatrists can provide counseling sessions, but many spend most of their time managing medications. These visits are usually brief. If it is a very brief visit for the sole purpose of monitoring or changing a patient's medication, the HCPCS code M0064 should be used.

On January 1, 2013 the other mental health codes were changed. For example previously a new patient initial psychiatric visit was the same as an initial visit for a social worker or psychologist. CPT code 90801 was used. But as of January 1, 2013 codes 90791 and 90792 are used.

There also used to be a specific CPT code 90862 for medication management. 90862 has been deleted and now E&M codes 99201-99215 are used. If counseling is done then there are add on codes that should be used. So, for example if a provider sees an established patient for a visit that meets the guidelines for a 99213 and they also perform 20 minutes of counseling, they would bill a 99213 and a 90832.

The code M0064 is for a very brief office visit to monitor or change drug prescriptions and is often used for nursing home visits. The visits are 10 minutes or less in length and involve a lesser level of drug monitoring or change than an E&M code.

The provider is responsible for documenting each visit in the patient's medical records. The notes must contain the clinical condition, if medication is adjusted or not, any side effects, and must be signed and dated by the provider.

There is a considerable difference in the reimbursement rates between the two codes. You can look up the allowable reimbursement rates for Medicare on their website.

Most commercial insurance plans do not require authorization for medication management but do for psychotherapy. Some plans do require authorization for both medication management and psychotherapy. Some may require a referral from the patient's PCP (primary care physician). Before a patient is seen for the first time the requirements should be checked out by verifying benefits with the insurance carrier. Verifying benefits, as the recordings state, are not a guarantee of benefits.

For those familiar with the old mental health CPT codes you can find many CPT crosswalks online. These crosswalks are very useful in converting to the new codes. One can be found at www.psychiatry.org/cptcodingchanges.

EAP Visits

Mental health billing is generally a fairly easy specialty to bill as far as medical insurance billing goes but EAP claims can make it quite a bit more involved. EAP or employee assistance programs are designed for employees with personal problems that might affect their work performance. They are becoming much more common than in the past.

Employees are referred to professional counselors who will assess the problem, provide short term counseling and if necessary refer the employee to additional resources. Many times the issues are resolved with a few sessions of counseling. Some states require that in order for a mental health professional to offer EAP services they must be credentialed as CEAP or certified employee assistance professional. State laws should be checked prior to seeing EAP patients.

In conjunction with EAP services are SAP or substance abuse professionals. These are counselors who work with employees who have violated a DOT (Department of Transportation) drug and alcohol regulation and must seek treatment. SAP counselors must complete training, pass an exam and become certified to treat patients. Employees who are ordered to see an SAP mental health provider may be required to attend a certain number of required sessions with ongoing follow-up testing.

Both EAP and SAP claims are usually billed to the insurance company very differently than regular commercial insurance claims. Sometimes special forms are required and specific procedure codes or modifiers are required. Usually an assessment of the visit is being reported with the claim and the counselor must complete this portion. EAP and SAP claims are not submitted to the employee's health insurance. Generally the claims are submitted to a separate carrier. The counselor should obtain this information from the patient who would get it from their Human Resources department.

Many times with an EAP case the situation can be resolved with just a few counseling sessions so it does not ever get billed to the patient's health insurance carrier. This provides the patient with more privacy and allows them to receive treatment for the situation without having the history of mental health treatment in their medical history since there is no link between the EAP claims and the major medical carrier. Some employers allow EAP's for the employee only, and some also will allow them for family members.

Many insurance carriers have information on their websites regarding billing EAP claims. When the counselor sets up the first appointment with the mental health provider, the representative of the insurance carrier should provide the instructions for billing for this particular patient. They may email or fax the instructions and forms to the provider or the provider may be referred to a website for instructions. These instructions must be followed carefully to insure payment. If a certain form is required then that form must be used or likely the claim will be denied.

Magellan is a large EAP insurer and has much information on their website about billing EAP insurance claims. They have the required forms, instructions, and contact information for EAP reimbursement. They also have an EAP Handbook supplement. All are available as a download in PDF. The websites can be a great resource to you in EAP billing.

The claims must also be submitted in whatever method the insurance carrier requests. It may state to fax the paperwork to a certain fax number or it may request that you mail the claim forms in. Make sure you check the mailing address if the claim is to be mailed. The address may be different than where you are used to sending standard CMS 1500 forms for commercial insurance claims.

Psychological & Neuropsychological Testing

Neuropsychological testing consists of specifically designed tasks used to measure a psychological function known to be linked to a particular brain structure or pathway. They are typically used to assess impairment after an injury or illness known to affect neurocognitive functioning.

Psychological testing consists of the use of samples of behavior in order to assess psychological construct(s), such as cognitive and emotional functioning, about a given patient. Neuropsychological testing consists of specifically designed tasks used to measure a psychological function known to be linked to a particular brain structure or pathway.

Licensed clinical psychologists, counseling psychologists and school psychologists are typically qualified to perform psychological assessments. The activity of these professionals is regulated by appropriate state statutes and licensing boards.

CPT codes for psychological testing did not change on January 1, 2013 and range from 96101 to 96103. CPT codes for neuropsychological testing range 96118-96120. These codes are each per hour of time, so the units would indicate the number of hours spent. Time would include both face-to-face with the patient and time spent interpreting results and preparing reports. Typically psychological or neuropsychological testing is between 6-8 hours on average.

Practice Management System

A good practice management system is almost a necessity for a medical office today. There is a huge quantity of information to keep track of even in a small office. It is important to keep track of all the claims that must be filed and the payments that are coming in. A practice management system will keep track of all patient demographic information, claims and both insurance and patient payments.

There are two different types of practice management systems, server based and web based. Server based software is one that is purchases and loaded directly onto the provider's computer. Once loaded a server based software does not change unless an update to the program is manually loaded. For example if a server based practice management program was purchased and loaded on your computer a year ago and now something new has been mandated such as the use of NPI#s or the change to ICD10 codes, the practice management system must be updated to allow for the updates. This means purchasing a newer or updated version.

Web based software is not purchased. Usually they charge a monthly fee for use of the software. The fee can vary based either on the number of providers or the number of computers. Web based software is usually updated automatically whenever changes are made. It also comes with many capabilities that server based software doesn't have such as real time changes. As codes or requirements change web based software is updated immediately while server based software requires the purchase of an updated program.

Most web based software offer a more detailed claims scrubber which catches problem claims before they are submitted to the carriers and denied. This enables a much better cash flow for the office. A claims scrubber checks over the claims before they are batched for submission. It looks for errors such as missing or invalid information allowing corrections to be made before the claims are sent on to the insurance carrier.

Practice Management Systems vary a lot in price and in functionality. For a mental health provider it isn't necessary to purchase a practice management system that costs $20,000 and has all the bells and whistles that a clinic or large medical office requires. But you also want to remember, you get what you pay for. So if you decide to go with a free software or a very inexpensive software, you may be limited in what you can do with it.

There are some companies that offer use of a free practice management system. They usually have limited functionality. They may do this to try to get you to upgrade to a version that you must pay for that has better functions.

Our personal experience with a free practice management system was that it requires so much more time to do the necessary work and it is so limited in what it can do that it just is not worth the time spent working in it. There are also software companies that make software for just mental health offices with just the functions that are needed in a mental health office. This type of software is usually less expensive.

A good practice management system will allow you to not only schedule your patients, but input your patient demographics, charges and payments. It should allow you to either print claims or submit them electronically. Today, electronic claims submission is almost impossible to avoid. Many carriers including Medicare have mandated electronic claims submission. There are ways to apply for a waiver to allow you to submit on paper, but it is getting harder to avoid.

Submitting claims electronically reduces the processing time, getting payment quicker, and makes it easier to track denied and unpaid claims, if it is a good system. But I'm getting ahead of myself. We'll talk more about submitting claims later.

Another important function of a practice management system is the reporting capabilities. The reporting capabilities will vary from practice management system to practice management system. It is important to be able to pull the reports that you will need - like insurance aging reports and patient aging reports. Those are needed to be able to make sure you are collecting everything that is due. Other reports like insurance analysis reports, transaction journal or monthly and yearly summaries are nice, but not required.

When deciding to purchase a practice management system make sure you research your decision. It is probably going to be one that you will have to live with for quite some time. Most people do not hop around from practice management system to practice management system. Make sure to choose one that will meet all of the needs and that is user friendly. This is not one of those items you want to make a rash decision on.

In our office we use Lytec for the providers when we work in our own practice management system. We do work with a few providers using their own web based programs. We have used Lytec for over 20 years and really like it for all kinds of different specialties. We have also used NowMD which is an inexpensive system and found it to work well for mental health.

Submitting the Claims

In order to receive reimbursement by an insurance carrier for a claim for mental health services, an insurance claim must be submitted to the carrier in CMS 1500 format either electronically or on a paper CMS 1500 (rev 02-12) form within a certain time frame of the visit. Claims can be denied for timely filing in as little as 45 days after the date of service.

It is important that they are filed quickly, correctly and with all the required information to the correct insurance carrier to prevent lost claims, denials and resubmissions. The best way to do this is to make sure you obtain good information from patients upfront.

- Make sure to get a photocopy of the front and back of the insurance card
- Have the patient complete an intake sheet.
- Make sure the proper authorizations and referrals are being done when required
- Make sure claims are coded correctly and appropriate modifiers are in place

Claims may be submitted to the insurance carriers on paper (CMS 1500 (rev 02-12) forms), electronically through your practice management system, or directly through some insurance carrier websites. If you plan on doing a lot of billing, it is much better to send them electronically as much as possible. It will prove to be less expensive and result in much quicker payments for the providers. Some of the smaller companies still are not capable of accepting electronic submissions, but most insurance carriers do.

If an authorization is required and an authorization number is assigned it should be placed in box 23 on the CMS 1500 form. If a referral is required the referring provider's name and individual NPI# should be in box 17 and 17a on the CMS 1500 form.

Submitting the claims for reimbursement is the second most important thing in an office. It is second only to treating the patients. A provider can treat the patients but if they are not paid for their services then they usually cannot continue unless they are independently wealthy and just treat patients for their own satisfaction. The mistake many providers make is in not recognizing the importance of the insurance billing. Having someone in charge who is knowledgeable in billing, whether the billing is done in house or outsourced to a good billing service is crucial. If a provider is doing the billing in house a system is a necessity to track claims and payments.

If submitting claims on paper, the CMS 1500 forms should be mailed to the address on the back of the patient's insurance ID card. If submitting claims electronically, you should check with the clearinghouse to get the correct payer ID number for the insurance carrier. A payer ID number is usually a set of 5 digit characters usually numeric, sometimes letters that tell the clearinghouse which insurance carrier the claims should go to. The payer ID should be entered into the appropriate field in the practice management system. When the electronic batch of claims is created, the payer ID will let the clearinghouse know which insurance carrier the claim should be sent to.

Claim forms can be completed by hand or by typewriter but that is really not practical. Most insurance carriers use OCR scanners and do not accept handwritten claims anymore.

All patient information should be entered into the practice management system, including insurance information. Then all information about their visit should be entered including the date of the visit, the diagnosis or ICD10 code, and the procedure or CPT code. Then the claim can be submitted electronically or printed out onto a paper CMS 1500 (rev 02-12) form.

Tracking Claims

It is very important to have a good system in place to track your insurance claims. Most offices use a practice management system to accomplish this task. Without a proper tracking system in place, much money will be lost.

Most mental health providers will enter each patient visit into the software to submit the insurance claim or to bill a patient if they have no insurance. If the patient pays anything at the time of service, that information will also be added. The insurance claims will then be sent electronically or on paper to the insurance carriers.

When payment is made on the claim, this information is entered into the software and it is determined whether or not there is a remaining balance. If the patient has a copay, it should have been paid at the time of service. Possibly the patient didn't have the capability to pay at that time, so a statement must be sent. The patient may not have a copay, but a patient responsibility. Some insurance companies pay a percentage of an allowed amount and the patient is responsible for a percentage. The patient must then be billed for the remaining balance allowed by the insurance carrier.

If the patient has a secondary policy, the secondary insurance carrier must be billed. If the secondary claim is not submitted electronically but is sent on paper on a CMS 1500 form, a copy of the primary eob is attached to the claim and mailed to the carrier. When payment is received or denied by the secondary carrier, there may or may not still be a remaining balance to be billed to the patient.

With all these claims being sent, it is common that a few do not make it to completion. Even though a claim is submitted it doesn't mean the insurance carrier receives it or that it gets processed. The practice management system will have the capability to run a report called an insurance aging report to see what claims are outstanding that should be paid by now. The claims can be checked either online or by calling to find out why they have not been processed.

When checking on outstanding claims, it is very likely some will be 'not on file.' It isn't worth wondering what happened to them, or arguing with the customer service representative about where they went. It is not unusual for 20 claims to be sent in the same envelope or in the same electronic batch and only 19 to be received and processed. Bottom line is that the claim needs to be paid and if the insurance carrier doesn't have it, further action must be taken.

There is just a certain percentage of claims that 'get lost'. Even when submitted electronically there are many things that can go wrong. Most claims are accounted for thru the electronic reports, but occasional something happens where a claim is just inexplicably 'lost'. Don't get hung up on it, just resubmit.

Occasionally a payment is made on a claim but no eob is received. If you are a billing service the provider may have received the eob but did not provide you with a copy. If you are the provider, or in the provider's office, the payment may have been made to the wrong provider. In either case, you should ask the representative of the insurance carrier to whom the check was made payable, to what address was it mailed, and was it cashed. Finding out this information will help to get to the bottom of what happened to the payment.

If you are a billing service and payment was made to the provider, sent to the provider's office, and it was cashed, most likely the provider got the payment but didn't notify you. What we do in this case is notify the provider of the information and ask for verification that they did in fact receive the payment. If this only happens once in a while, we let it slide. But if it is common for the provider to get payments and not notify us then it is a problem as we are wasting our time on unnecessary phone calls.

Info for Billing Services

There is a lot of work involved with checking on an unpaid claim. The claim comes up on a report and either a phone call is made or an online inquiry is done. The information is gathered and reported to the provider. Then a response comes back from the provider. All of this work just because the provider didn't provide the eob. If they are a repeat offender, all of your profits are being eaten up. In some cases you may pay your employees more to do the work than you actually get from the provider.

If you are the provider or work for the provider and payment was made but you don't have any record of it, making sure it was paid to the correct provider is the first step. If the check was made out to the provider and mailed to the right address, then maybe it just wasn't recorded properly. Hopefully you have some sort of filing system for eobs that you will be able to verify that it was received. If after researching it you still don't show proof of the payment you can request a copy of the cancelled check from the insurance carrier.

Unfortunately some provider's offices have to deal with employee theft. It is a good idea to verify that the provider did receive the payment and the check was deposited into the office bank account to make sure it wasn't cashed without the provider's permission or knowledge.

We have seen instances where payment for services by one provider was made to a different provider by mistake. It doesn't happen often, but it does happen. That is why it is important to verify who the check was made out to and what address it was mailed to.

We have also seen where the check was made out correctly and mailed to the correct address, but wasn't cashed. Even though it was made out correctly and addressed correctly doesn't guarantee that something else didn't happen to it that prevented it from being delivered. Occasionally you hear stories of the post office finding mail from years ago that got 'misplaced'. Or the check could have gotten stuck to another check in the insurance carrier's check writing facility and mailed to the wrong provider even though it was made out correctly. That provider may have just shredded the check without notifying anyone.

In any case, if the check wasn't cashed the insurance carrier will issue a new one. They all have different rules on how much time must pass before they reissue. Most require 30 days must pass before they will reissue the check.

When checking status some claims will have been denied for some reason but no notice was received. Sometimes they mail notice to the patient or policy holder, sometimes they don't send anything. They will usually will advise you of the reason during the phone call unless the provider is non participating. Many times if the provider is non participating they will not discuss the claim.

Again, don't get hung up on the fact that you didn't get the notice. It doesn't do any good in getting the claim paid. But do take notes on the name of the representative and what they advised you. This may come in handy later on if an appeal needs to be filed.

Do what must be done to find out the reason for the denial and what needs to be done to get the claim paid if possible. If the claim was denied for a reason that cannot be fixed or appealed and the patient is responsible, get a bill out as soon as possible. Patients don't like to be billed long after services were received. Also, the chance of getting paid is greater the closer it is to the date of service.

In some cases the claim may have been denied incorrectly by the insurance carrier. If this is the case it usually becomes evident during the conversation. If the claim was denied but the reason does not make sense, ask the customer service representative to explain. Many times they will recognize that the denial was incorrect and will send the claim back for adjustment.

An example of this may be that a claim was denied stating there was no authorization for the treatment but you show an authorization on file. The customer service representative will check the authorization and may determine that you are correct and that the services should not have been denied.

In this case they will usually reprocess the claim. They may request that the claim be resubmitted. Personally, I would argue as to why they need the claim resubmitted if they have the denied claim on file and the mistake was on their end. But again, the bottom line is getting the claim paid, so I would do whatever was required to accomplish that.

Once a claim has been paid in full, meaning that payment has been collected from any insurance companies and/or patient payments, make sure the balance on the claim is zeroed out - meaning that the entire amount of the claim has been accounted for. If the insurance did not allow the full amount charged make sure the contractual adjustment was recorded. Make sure all payments, both insurance and patient payments, have been applied. It can mess up the system to leave balances on an account if nothing is truly owed.

Insurance Payments

Once claims have been filed or submitted to the insurance carriers payments will start to arrive. Some carriers pay claims in as little as 7 to 10 days if the claims were filed electronically. Paper claims can be paid in as little as 2 to 3 weeks for the quicker insurance carriers. Medicare electronic claims are paid in 14 days with the funds being direct deposited into the provider's bank account.

Some insurance carriers have electronic remittance advices or ERA's instead of the paper eobs, or explanation of benefit statements. Many practice management systems allow the ERA's to be posted automatically which saves a lot of time. Instead of having to manually post the payments they are automatically posted to the practice management system from the ERA.

Whether the payments are received by direct deposit or by check, or whether there is a paper eob or an ERA, it is important that the payments get posted properly. In addition to posting the payment there may be a contractual adjustment, or an amount that was disallowed by the insurance carrier. If the provider is participating they must write this amount off, or apply the contractual adjustment. If there is a patient responsibility that was not paid at the time of service, the patient must be billed.

If the patient has multiple insurance policies then the secondary or tertiary policy may need to be billed. When posting an insurance payment it is important to make sure the appropriate insurance payment is being indicated. For example, if a payment from the primary insurance policy is being posted, then the payment should reflect that it is a primary insurance payment. If the payment is from the patient's secondary policy, then the payment should reflect that.

For example, in our practice management system we post primary insurance payments using the code 'IP' for 'insurance payment'. For a secondary payment we use 'SIP' for 'secondary insurance payment' and 'TIP' for 'tertiary insurance payment'. It is important that the practice management system know which insurance the payment is for so that it can track which policy still owes payment on a claim. Some practice management systems have you actually select the insurance carrier who made the payment.

If a patient has Medicare prime and BCBS secondary and payment is received from Medicare, it should be recorded as a primary insurance payment and a secondary claim should be filed to BCBS. If it is recorded properly then the practice management system will know that payment from Medicare was received and now the provider is waiting for payment from BCBS. If the BCBS payment comes in and it is recorded as a primary insurance payment, then the practice management system will still think that BCBS owes money on the claim.

Actually you can go much further than this and enter primary insurance payments with a code for the insurance company that paid such as MCRPMT could mean Medicare primary payment while MCR2PMT indicates Medicare secondary payment. The same could be done for contractual adjustments such as MCRADJ. This type of entry can be very beneficial in running reports and finding specific problems.

Failing to record payments properly can cause a lot of problems down the road. Aging reports may not be accurate and money can be lost. Balances in the computer may not be accurate.

Secondary and Tertiary Claims

When we first started our medical billing business in 1994 I had no previous experience at billing any medical claims, let alone secondary and tertiary. (You mean some people have 3 insurances?) I knew nothing. In twenty two years of billing I've learned quite a bit and I see from questions in our forum that many beginners do not understand secondary and tertiary claims billing at all.

First of all, how does anyone get two or three policies and which is determined primary? If a husband and a wife both work (who doesn't?) and they are both covered by health insurance by their employers, they may both have family policies so they are both covered under each other's plan. One would be primary and the other secondary. Now if one of this couple had previous military experience and carried over their Tricare military insurance, that would be the third payer (if there was a balance left).

Which company is primary and which one is secondary is determined by one of a couple different methods. First of all, if a person is working and they carry insurance, that insurance is primary (unless they have Medicare and their employer has less than 100 employees). If a person is retired and has Medicare but the spouse works and carries a family policy, then the spouse's plan would be primary and the Medicare would be secondary.

There is no way to cover every scenario but basically whether or not the person or the spouse is working can determine the order. For dependants (usually children) some go by the "birthday rule" meaning that whichever parents birthday falls first in the year is primary. Of course with all of the divorce out there sometimes the order of insurance is determined by a court order.

This process of determining which policy is prime is called coordination of benefits or COB and is determined by the insurance companies. Sometimes claims will be denied as the insurance carrier has not yet received a COB form from the patient so they could determine who is primary and who is secondary.

Once the primary insurance carrier pays their share of the claim it is then submitted to the secondary insurance company if the patient has one. Secondary claims can also be sent electronically or on paper. Medicare is mandating electronic submissions even on secondary claims. When submitted electronically all the information from the eob (explanation of benefits) is entered into the claim information and submitted to the secondary insurance carrier in electronic format.

When the secondary claim is submitted on paper, the claim is printed out again on a CMS form indicating the secondary insurance policy information and a photocopy of the eob from the primary insurance company is attached. If your eob is in the form of an era you may have the capability of printing out just the one payment on that eob that you need for your secondary claim.

If other patients are listed on the eob, their personal information should be hidden. Many offices use black markers (we call them smelly pens) to draw through the unwanted information. The problem with the black markers is that they don't always cover the information. Sometimes when the ink dries the information is still visible. If you are going to cross off the information with black pen make sure it is no longer able to be read.

Some offices photocopy the eob and then cut out the ones that need to be submitted to secondary carriers and re-photocopy them on their own sheet of paper. We have a set of white cardboard strips of various widths that we slide into a clear plastic sleeve to cover all of the unwanted information, allowing us to photocopy just the desired information to attach to the secondary claim.

The problem with each of the above methods is the amount of time it takes to create the copy needed to submit the claim. It is important that you figure out which method works best for your office, and takes the least amount of time. Secondary claims are important, but you can't afford to take so much time to create the eob copy that other jobs suffer.

If there is still a balance after the secondary insurance carrier pays their share, the claim is sent on to the third carrier. It is printed out again on a CMS form and copies of the eobs of both the primary and the secondary insurance carriers are attached.

Whenever you send secondary and tertiary claims on paper, make sure the photocopies you attach are clear, easy to read, and for the correct date of service. Many insurance carriers scan the eobs which lightens them a little. If the copy you submitted was already light, by the time the claim is processed it may be sent back to you as unreadable. It takes a lot more time to find the original eob and resubmit a claim than it does to get it right the first time.

Secondary and tertiary claims can sometimes seem like a pain to get paid – especially because they can be for a very small amount of money. It is still important to file and track these claims to keep your receivables under control. It may not seem like a lot of money but it adds up. If you have a system for submitting them it really isn't that bad. It also helps to have a good filing system for the eobs so you can go back and find one again when you find you need to resubmit.

With today's technology many offices choose to scan the eobs and store them on the computer. This can make finding an eob much easier and cut down on space required for filing. Whatever method you use just make sure you set up a system that works for you.

Denials and Appeals

One of the most difficult tasks in the medical office for the billing department is dealing with insurance denials. Unfortunately many claims are denied for a variety of reasons and if not handled properly no payment will ever be made on that service. Most offices are extremely busy and it can be difficult to find the time to take care of these problems. If this task is not handled properly the receivables will greatly suffer.

Denials can range from no coverage to treatment notes needed. Each individual denial needs to be looked into to determine how you will get paid for that date of service. Many times it will take only a phone call to fix the problem, but that phone call can take as long as 45 minutes to accomplish the preferred outcome.

Some denials will entail the resubmission of the claim. An incorrect diagnosis code is an example of this. Some denials will result in billing the patient for the service but it may still take a 30 minute phone call to be sure that you are doing the right thing.

The secret to handling denials effectively is to act as soon as possible on the denial. Many denials have a time frame that must be adhered to. For example, some insurance carriers only allow 60 days from the date the claim was processed to file an appeal.

Next you need a good system in place for dealing with the denial. When a claim is denied find what works best for that problem and use the same method each time you get that denial. Find the most effective solution to each denial and use that solution as soon as you receive the denial.

For instance, when we get a denial for no coverage found on patient, the first thing that we do is determine if this was the first claim for the patient. If we have had claims paid already, then maybe there was a mistake at the insurance carrier. If this is the initial visit, then we would check the intake information to make sure there wasn't a mistake in the data entry. If there was no mistake or if claims had been paid in history then we make a call to the insurance carrier to verify that the denial is correct. It may just be that the ID# has recently changed.

If they do verify that the patient does not have coverage then the patient would need to be billed. Coverage should have been verified prior to the treatment but sometimes it still can be terminated between the time it was verified and the time the claim was received.

If a claim is denied for an incorrect ID# we determine what we do based on the insurance carrier. Some insurance carriers allow you to look up ID numbers on their website. If you are a billing service you may have to contact your provider and ask them to get the correct ID from the patient when they come in. A bill can be sent out to the patient asking for updated insurance information. As you gain experience you will determine the best way for you to correct the problem.

If a claim is denied for no coverage the patient should be contacted as soon as possible to see if this is accurate. Did they lose their coverage or did the information just change? The longer it takes to get the correct information and get the claim rebilled, the less likely the claim will eventually be paid.

When claims are denied for the diagnosis it may be for a couple different reasons. A claim may be denied for invalid diagnosis. Take a look at that diagnosis in a current ICD10 list and see if it is valid. It may require a more specific code, it may be outdated, or it may be totally wrong. Some claims are denied for the diagnosis codes being in the wrong order. The patient's chart must be checked or the provider must be notified of any diagnosis problems.

Make sure you document your actions. A month later a question may arise about this claim and if you didn't make a note in the computer, you can't be sure of what you did previously. The provider may ask what is going on with this claim. You want to be able to say that on such and such a day you did this and then on such and such a day you did that.

Sometimes denials are completely incorrect. Usually a phone call to the insurance company can resolve the problem. We sometimes have claims rejected at the edit stage of an electronic submission for no insurance coverage. A call to the insurance company or sometimes checking their website may tell us that the prefix of the identification number has changed. We change the prefix and resubmit the claim. Or we may have made a typo in the ID# that needs to be corrected.

We have had claims that were accepted, but applied to the deductible. After the patient was billed we received a call from the patient stating that they either don't have a deductible or that it has already been met. Sometimes the patient is wrong and sometimes the insurance company is wrong, but all these challenges must be dealt with if you in order to receive payment. The more you delay in dealing with the problems, the better the chances are that you will not be paid.

When a denial is received that is not understood, call the insurance carrier and ask them to explain it. Just make sure there is a policy of handling denials as soon as they come in. You will learn what is the best way to handle each one. Just make sure they get taken care of as soon as possible.

For more information on denials and appeals refer to our book "Denials, Appeals and Adjustments."

Patient Portion

Most insurance policies require a copay or patient responsibility to be paid by the patient. It is very important that your providers collect the patient payments as well as the insurance payments. When a provider participates with an insurance carrier he or she is signing a contract that they are breaking if they do not make an attempt to collect the patient portion.

Copays are due at the time of service and coinsurance is usually determined after payment by the insurance carrier. Coinsurance is usually a percentage of the amount allowed by the insurance carrier and can involve a deductible.

When billing the patients it is important to make sure the billing goes out regularly. Implement some sort system so patient billing is done monthly. There is a much better chance of getting paid when patient statements are sent on a regular basis

We run our patient billing for each account once a month. We send three bills – the first is a clear statement of the account indicating the reason they are responsible – i.e. copay, coinsurance, deductible, or denial reason. The second one is sent a month later as a second notice indicating that we have not heard from them regarding their past due balance. The third is a final notice. If the bill is not acted upon within 10 days this will be sent to a collection agency.

A phone number should be printed on the bill as to who should be called in case the patient needs to speak to someone regarding the balance. It also helps to include a return envelope with the bill. Patients are more likely to pay a bill when a return envelope is included. It doesn't require a great expense. Small envelopes may be purchased from an office supply store near you or ordered online, and address labels can be attached with the provider's address. It doesn't cost much, but it will save on future bills or even collection costs.

Filing insurance claims and getting full reimbursement has become more complicated and time consuming over the past several years. Things are always changing in this field requiring changes for the providers.

Billing for mental health providers is very similar to billing for all other specialties in many ways. The patient comes in, information is gathered, a claim is submitted and tracked and payment is received. There are many things that affect this process and it's important to understand all of the aspects to ensure proper payment. There are some aspects that are more common with mental health than some specialties such as authorizations and referrals.

It is important to understand the different types of insurances and how provider participation affects payment. Many mental health visits occur in a private office, but some occur in facilities such as nursing homes and assisted living facilities. The same CPT or procedure codes are used for these visits but the appropriate place of service code must be used to indicate the setting. Currently ICD10 codes are used to report the diagnoses for the services.

Submitting the claims can be done electronically or on paper. Once submitted the claims must be tracked until payment is received. Insurance payments must be posted correctly and patients must be billed for any patient responsibility. It is also important to handle denials quickly. Getting systems in place for all billing tasks is crucial.

1500

HEALTH INSURANCE CLAIM FORM

APPROVED BY NATIONAL UNIFORM CLAIM COMMITTEE (NUCC) 02/12

Aetna
P O Box 55447
El Paso TX 67554

☐☐☐ PICA   PICA ☐☐☐

1. MEDICARE	MEDICAID	TRICARE	CHAMPVA	GROUP HEALTH PLAN	FECA BLK LUNG	OTHER	1a. INSURED'S I.D. NUMBER (For Program in Item 1)
(Medicare #)	(Medicaid #)	(Sponsor's SSN)	(Member ID#) X	(SSN or ID)	(SSN)	(ID)	W116657422

2. PATIENT'S NAME (Last Name, First Name, Middle Initial)
Clark, Benjamin, E

3. PATIENT'S BIRTH DATE   MM 03 DD 26 YY 1975   SEX M X   F ☐

4. INSURED'S NAME (Last Name, First Name, Middle Initial)
Clark, Benjamin, E

5. PATIENT'S ADDRESS (No., Street)
568 Main St

6. PATIENT RELATIONSHIP TO INSURED
Self X   Spouse ☐   Child ☐   Other ☐

7. INSURED'S ADDRESS (No., Street)
568 Main St

CITY Boonville   STATE NY

8. RESERVED FOR NUCC USE

CITY Boonville   STATE NY

ZIP CODE 13309   TELEPHONE (Include Area Code)

ZIP CODE 13309   TELEPHONE (Include Area Code)

9. OTHER INSURED'S NAME (Last Name, First Name, Middle Initial)

10. IS PATIENT'S CONDITION RELATED TO:

11. INSURED'S POLICY GROUP OR FECA NUMBER

a. OTHER INSURED'S POLICY OR GROUP NUMBER

a. EMPLOYMENT? (Current or Previous)
☐ YES   X NO

a. INSURED'S DATE OF BIRTH   MM 03 DD 26 YY 1975   SEX M X   F ☐

b. RESERVED FOR NUCC USE

b. AUTO ACCIDENT?   PLACE (State)
☐ YES   X NO

b. OTHER CLAIM ID (Designated by NUCC)

c. RESERVED FOR NUCC USE

c. OTHER ACCIDENT?
☐ YES   X NO

c. INSURANCE PLAN NAME OR PROGRAM NAME
Aetna

d. INSURANCE PLAN NAME OR PROGRAM NAME

10d. CLAIM CODES (Designated by NUCC)

d. IS THERE ANOTHER HEALTH BENEFIT PLAN?
☐ YES   X NO   If yes, complete items 9, 9a, and 9d.

READ BACK OF FORM BEFORE COMPLETING & SIGNING THIS FORM

12. PATIENT'S OR AUTHORIZED PERSON'S SIGNATURE I authorize the release of any medical or other information necessary to process this claim. I also request payment of government benefits either to myself or to the party who accepts assignment below.
SIGNED Signature on file   DATE 01 12 2016

13. INSURED'S OR AUTHORIZED PERSON'S SIGNATURE I authorize payment of medical benefits to the undersigned physician or supplier for services described below.
SIGNED Signature on file

14. DATE OF CURRENT ILLNESS, INJURY, or PREGNANCY (LMP) MM DD YY   QUAL.

15. OTHER DATE   QUAL.   MM DD YY

16. DATES PATIENT UNABLE TO WORK IN CURRENT OCCUPATION   MM DD YY   FROM   TO   MM DD YY

17. NAME OF REFERRING PHYSICIAN OR OTHER SOURCE
17a.
17b. NPI

18. HOSPITALIZATION DATES RELATED TO CURRENT SERVICES   MM DD YY   FROM   TO   MM DD YY

19. ADDITIONAL CLAIM INFORMATION (Designated by NUCC)

20. OUTSIDE LAB? $ CHARGES
☐ YES   X NO

21. DIAGNOSIS OR NATURE OF ILLNESS OR INJURY. (Relate A-L to service line below (24E))   ICD Ind. 9

A. | B. | C. | D.
E. | F. | G. | H.
I. | J. | K. | L.

22. RESUBMISSION CODE   ORIGINAL REF. NO.

23. PRIOR AUTHORIZATION NUMBER

24. A. DATE(S) OF SERVICE From MM DD YY To MM DD YY	B. PLACE OF SERVICE	C. EMG	D. PROCEDURES, SERVICES, OR SUPPLIES (Explain Unusual Circumstances) CPT/HCPCS MODIFIER	E. DIAGNOSIS POINTER	F. $ CHARGES	G. DAYS OR UNITS	H. EPSDT Family Plan	I. ID. QUAL.	J. RENDERING PROVIDER ID. #
09 06 15 09 06 15	11	N	90791	A	225 00	1		NPI	1700838596
								NPI	
								NPI	
								NPI	
								NPI	
								NPI	

25. FEDERAL TAX I.D. NUMBER   SSN EIN
123456789   X

26. PATIENT'S ACCOUNT NO.
21

27. ACCEPT ASSIGNMENT? (For govt. claims, see back)
X YES   ☐ NO

28. TOTAL CHARGE $ 225 00

29. AMOUNT PAID $ 0 00

30. Rsvd for NUCC Use

31. SIGNATURE OF PHYSICIAN OR SUPPLIER INCLUDING DEGREES OR CREDENTIALS (I certify that the statements on the reverse apply to this bill and are made a part thereof.)
ul Scott DC
SIGNED   DATE 01 12 2016

32. SERVICE FACILITY LOCATION INFORMATION
Middleville Healthcare
466 Black River Blvd
Rome NY 13440
a. 1285692673   b.

33. BILLING PROVIDER INFO & PH #   315 337 3000
Middleville Healthcare
466 Black River Blvd
Rome NY 13440
a. 1285692673   b.

NUCC Instruction Manual available at: www.nucc.org   PLEASE PRINT OR TYPE   APPROVED OMB-0938-1197 FORM 1500 (02-12)

1500

HEALTH INSURANCE CLAIM FORM

APPROVED BY NATIONAL UNIFORM CLAIM COMMITTEE (NUCC) 02/12

Aetna
P O Box 55447
El Paso TX 67554

| | PICA | | | | | | | | PICA |

| 1. MEDICARE (Medicare #) | MEDICAID (Medicaid #) | TRICARE (Sponsor's SSN) | CHAMPVA (Member ID#) | GROUP HEALTH PLAN (SSN or ID) **X** | FECA BLK LUNG (SSN) | OTHER (ID) | 1a. INSURED'S I.D. NUMBER (For Program in Item 1) W741698305 |

2. PATIENT'S NAME (Last Name, First Name, Middle Initial)
Jeffries, Mary

3. PATIENT'S BIRTH DATE MM 05 DD 06 YY 1975 — SEX M / F **X**

4. INSURED'S NAME (Last Name, First Name, Middle Initial)
Jeffries, Mary

5. PATIENT'S ADDRESS (No., Street)
P O Box 45

6. PATIENT RELATIONSHIP TO INSURED
Self **X** Spouse Child Other

7. INSURED'S ADDRESS (No., Street)
P O Box 45

CITY Rome — STATE NY

8. RESERVED FOR NUCC USE

CITY Rome — STATE NY

ZIP CODE 13440 — TELEPHONE (Include Area Code)

ZIP CODE 13440 — TELEPHONE (Include Area Code)

9. OTHER INSURED'S NAME (Last Name, First Name, Middle Initial)

10. IS PATIENT'S CONDITION RELATED TO:

11. INSURED'S POLICY GROUP OR FECA NUMBER

a. OTHER INSURED'S POLICY OR GROUP NUMBER

a. EMPLOYMENT? (Current or Previous)
YES **X** NO

a. INSURED'S DATE OF BIRTH MM 05 DD 06 YY 1975 — SEX M / F **X**

b. RESERVED FOR NUCC USE

b. AUTO ACCIDENT? PLACE (State)
YES **X** NO

b. OTHER CLAIM ID (Designated by NUCC)

c. RESERVED FOR NUCC USE

c. OTHER ACCIDENT?
YES **X** NO

c. INSURANCE PLAN NAME OR PROGRAM NAME
Aetna

d. INSURANCE PLAN NAME OR PROGRAM NAME

10d. CLAIM CODES (Designated by NUCC)

d. IS THERE ANOTHER HEALTH BENEFIT PLAN?
YES **X** NO If yes, complete items 9, 9a, and 9d.

READ BACK OF FORM BEFORE COMPLETING & SIGNING THIS FORM

12. PATIENT'S OR AUTHORIZED PERSON'S SIGNATURE I authorize the release of any medical or other information necessary to process this claim. I also request payment of government benefits either to myself or to the party who accepts assignment below.

SIGNED Signature on file DATE 01 12 2016

13. INSURED'S OR AUTHORIZED PERSON'S SIGNATURE I authorize payment of medical benefits to the undersigned physician or supplier for services described below.

SIGNED Signature on file

14. DATE OF CURRENT ILLNESS, INJURY, or PREGNANCY (LMP) MM DD YY QUAL.

15. OTHER DATE QUAL. MM DD YY

16. DATES PATIENT UNABLE TO WORK IN CURRENT OCCUPATION FROM MM DD YY TO MM DD YY

17. NAME OF REFERRING PHYSICIAN OR OTHER SOURCE

17a.
17b. NPI

18. HOSPITALIZATION DATES RELATED TO CURRENT SERVICES FROM MM DD YY TO MM DD YY

19. ADDITIONAL CLAIM INFORMATION (Designated by NUCC)

20. OUTSIDE LAB? YES **X** NO $ CHARGES

21. DIAGNOSIS OR NATURE OF ILLNESS OR INJURY. (Relate A-L to service line below (24E)) ICD Ind. 0

A. F411 B. C. D.
E. F. G. H.
I. J. K. L.

22. RESUBMISSION CODE ORIGINAL REF. NO.

23. PRIOR AUTHORIZATION NUMBER

24. A. DATE(S) OF SERVICE From MM DD YY	To MM DD YY	B. PLACE OF SERVICE	C. EMG	D. PROCEDURES, SERVICES, OR SUPPLIES (Explain Unusual Circumstances) CPT/HCPCS	MODIFIER	E. DIAGNOSIS POINTER	F. $ CHARGES	G. DAYS OR UNITS	H. EPSDT Family Plan	I. ID. QUAL.	J. RENDERING PROVIDER ID. #
10 04 15	10 04 15	11	N	90834		A	100 00	1		NPI	1386713956
										NPI	
										NPI	
										NPI	
										NPI	
										NPI	

25. FEDERAL TAX I.D. NUMBER SSN EIN
123456789 **X**

26. PATIENT'S ACCOUNT NO. 22

27. ACCEPT ASSIGNMENT? (For govt. claims, see back) **X** YES NO

28. TOTAL CHARGE $ 100 00

29. AMOUNT PAID $ 0 00

30. Rsvd for NUCC

31. SIGNATURE OF PHYSICIAN OR SUPPLIER INCLUDING DEGREES OR CREDENTIALS (I certify that the statements on the reverse apply to this bill and are made a part thereof.)
Roger Karam LCSW
SIGNED 01 12 2016 DATE

32. SERVICE FACILITY LOCATION INFORMATION
Middleville Healthcare
466 Black River Blvd
Rome NY 13440
a. 1285692673 b.

33. BILLING PROVIDER INFO & PH # 315 337 3000
Middleville Healthcare
466 Black River Blvd
Rome NY 13440
a. 1285692673 b.

NUCC Instruction Manual available at: www.nucc.org   PLEASE PRINT OR TYPE   APPROVED OMB-0938-1197 FORM 1500 (

1500

HEALTH INSURANCE CLAIM FORM

APPROVED BY NATIONAL UNIFORM CLAIM COMMITTEE (NUCC) 02/12

Aetna
P O Box 55447
El Paso TX 67554

| | PICA | | | | | | | | PICA | |

1. MEDICARE	MEDICAID	TRICARE	CHAMPVA	GROUP HEALTH PLAN	FECA BLK LUNG	OTHER	1a. INSURED'S I.D. NUMBER	(For Program in Item 1)
(Medicare #)	(Medicaid #)	(Sponsor's SSN)	(Member ID# X	(SSN or ID)	(SSN)	(ID)	W741698305	

2. PATIENT'S NAME (Last Name, First Name, Middle Initial)
Jeffries, Sally

3. PATIENT'S BIRTH DATE MM 06 DD 15 YY 1994 **SEX** M ☐ F ☒

4. INSURED'S NAME (Last Name, First Name, Middle Initial)
Jeffries, Mary

5. PATIENT'S ADDRESS (No., Street)
P O Box 45

6. PATIENT RELATIONSHIP TO INSURED Self ☐ Spouse ☐ Child ☒ Other ☐

7. INSURED'S ADDRESS (No., Street)
P O Box 45

CITY Rome STATE NY

8. RESERVED FOR NUCC USE

CITY Rome STATE NY

ZIP CODE 13440 TELEPHONE (Include Area Code)

ZIP CODE 13440 TELEPHONE (Include Area Code)

9. OTHER INSURED'S NAME (Last Name, First Name, Middle Initial

10. IS PATIENT'S CONDITION RELATED TO:

11. INSURED'S POLICY GROUP OR FECA NUMBER

a. OTHER INSURED'S POLICY OR GROUP NUMBER

a. EMPLOYMENT? (Current or Previous) YES ☐ NO ☒

a. INSURED'S DATE OF BIRTH MM 05 DD 06 YY 1975 SEX M ☐ F ☒

b. RESERVED FOR NUCC USE

b. AUTO ACCIDENT? PLACE (State) YES ☐ NO ☒

b. OTHER CLAIM ID (Designated by NUCC)

c. RESERVED FOR NUCC USE

c. OTHER ACCIDENT? YES ☐ NO ☒

c. INSURANCE PLAN NAME OR PROGRAM NAME
Aetna

d. INSURANCE PLAN NAME OR PROGRAM NAME

10d. CLAIM CODES (Designated by NUCC)

d. IS THERE ANOTHER HEALTH BENEFIT PLAN? YES ☐ NO ☒ **If yes,** complete items 9, 9a, and 9d.

READ BACK OF FORM BEFORE COMPLETING & SIGNING THIS FORM

12. PATIENT'S OR AUTHORIZED PERSON'S SIGNATURE I authorize the release of any medical or other information necessary to process this claim. I also request payment of government benefits either to myself or to the party who accepts assignment below.

SIGNED Signature on file DATE 01 12 2016

13. INSURED'S OR AUTHORIZED PERSON'S SIGNATURE I authorize payment of medical benefits to the undersigned physician or supplier for services described below.

SIGNED Signature on file

14. DATE OF CURRENT ILLNESS, INJURY, or PREGNANCY (LMP) MM DD YY QUAL.

15. OTHER DATE QUAL. MM DD YY

16. DATES PATIENT UNABLE TO WORK IN CURRENT OCCUPATION MM DD YY FROM TO MM DD YY

17. NAME OF REFERRING PHYSICIAN OR OTHER SOURCE 17a. 17b. NPI

18. HOSPITALIZATION DATES RELATED TO CURRENT SERVICES MM DD YY FROM TO MM DD YY

19. ADDITIONAL CLAIM INFORMATION (Designated by NUCC)

20. OUTSIDE LAB? YES ☐ NO ☒ $ CHARGES

21. DIAGNOSIS OR NATURE OF ILLNESS OR INJURY. (Relate A-L, to service line below (24E) ICD Ind. 0

A. F4325 B. C. D.
E. F. G. H.
I. J. K. L.

22. RESUBMISSION CODE ORIGINAL REF. NO.

23. PRIOR AUTHORIZATION NUMBER

A. DATE(S) OF SERVICE From			To			B. PLACE OF SERVICE	C. EMG	D. PROCEDURES, SERVICES, OR SUPPLIES (Explain Unusual Circumstances) CPT/HCPCS	MODIFIER	E. DIAGNOSIS POINTER	F. $ CHARGES		G. DAYS OR UNITS	H. EPSDT Family Plan	I. ID. QUAL.	J. RENDERING PROVIDER ID. #
MM 10	DD 02	YY 15	MM 10	DD 02	YY 15	11	N	90834		A	100	00	1		NPI	1386713956
															NPI	
															NPI	
															NPI	
															NPI	
															NPI	

25. FEDERAL TAX I.D. NUMBER SSN ☐ EIN ☒
123456789

26. PATIENT'S ACCOUNT NO.
23

27. ACCEPT ASSIGNMENT? (For govt. claims, see back) YES ☒ NO ☐

28. TOTAL CHARGE $ 100 00

29. AMOUNT PAID $ 0 00

30. Rsvd for NUCC Use

31. SIGNATURE OF PHYSICIAN OR SUPPLIER INCLUDING DEGREES OR CREDENTIALS (I certify that the statements on the reverse apply to this bill and are made a part thereof.)
ger Karam LCSW
01 12 2016
SIGNED DATE

32. SERVICE FACILITY LOCATION INFORMATION
Middleville Healthcare
466 Black River Blvd
Rome NY 13440
a. 1285692673 b.

33. BILLING PROVIDER INFO & PH # 315 337 3000
Middleville Healthcare
466 Black River Blvd
Rome NY 13440
a. 1285692673 b.

NUCC Instruction Manual available at: www.nucc.org PLEASE PRINT OR TYPE APPROVED OMB-0938-1197 FORM 1500 (02-12)

1500

HEALTH INSURANCE CLAIM FORM

APPROVED BY NATIONAL UNIFORM CLAIM COMMITTEE (NUCC) 02/12

Aetna
P O Box 55447
El Paso TX 67554

| | PICA | | | | | | | PICA |

1. MEDICARE	MEDICAID	TRICARE	CHAMPVA	GROUP HEALTH PLAN	FECA BLK LUNG	OTHER	1a. INSURED'S I.D. NUMBER (For Program in Item 1)
(Medicare #)	(Medicaid #)	(Sponsor's SSN)	(Member ID#) X	(SSN or ID)	(SSN)	(ID)	W741698305

2. PATIENT'S NAME (Last Name, First Name, Middle Initial)	3. PATIENT'S BIRTH DATE	SEX	4. INSURED'S NAME (Last Name, First Name, Middle Initial)
Jeffries, Travis	MM 10 DD 14 YY 1999 M X F		Jeffries, Mary

5. PATIENT'S ADDRESS (No., Street)	6. PATIENT RELATIONSHIP TO INSURED	7. INSURED'S ADDRESS (No., Street)
P O Box 45	Self ☐ Spouse ☐ Child X Other ☐	P O Box 45
CITY Rome	STATE NY	8. RESERVED FOR NUCC USE	CITY Rome	STATE NY
ZIP CODE 13440	TELEPHONE (Include Area Code)		ZIP CODE 13440	TELEPHONE (Include Area Code)

9. OTHER INSURED'S NAME (Last Name, First Name, Middle Initial)	10. IS PATIENT'S CONDITION RELATED TO:	11. INSURED'S POLICY GROUP OR FECA NUMBER
a. OTHER INSURED'S POLICY OR GROUP NUMBER	a. EMPLOYMENT? (Current or Previous) ☐ YES X NO	a. INSURED'S DATE OF BIRTH MM 05 DD 06 YY 1975 SEX M ☐ F X
b. RESERVED FOR NUCC USE	b. AUTO ACCIDENT? PLACE (State) ☐ YES X NO	b. OTHER CLAIM ID (Designated by NUCC)
c. RESERVED FOR NUCC USE	c. OTHER ACCIDENT? ☐ YES X NO	c. INSURANCE PLAN NAME OR PROGRAM NAME Aetna
d. INSURANCE PLAN NAME OR PROGRAM NAME	10d. CLAIM CODES (Designated by NUCC)	d. IS THERE ANOTHER HEALTH BENEFIT PLAN? ☐ YES X NO If yes, complete items 9, 9a, and 9d.

READ BACK OF FORM BEFORE COMPLETING & SIGNING THIS FORM

12. PATIENT'S OR AUTHORIZED PERSON'S SIGNATURE I authorize the release of any medical or other information necessary to process this claim. I also request payment of government benefits either to myself or to the party who accepts assignment below.

SIGNED Signature on file   DATE 01 12 2016

13. INSURED'S OR AUTHORIZED PERSON'S SIGNATURE I authorize payment of medical benefits to the undersigned physician or supplier for services described below.

SIGNED Signature on file

14. DATE OF CURRENT ILLNESS, INJURY, or PREGNANCY (LMP) MM DD YY QUAL.	15. OTHER DATE QUAL. MM DD YY	16. DATES PATIENT UNABLE TO WORK IN CURRENT OCCUPATION FROM MM DD YY TO MM DD YY
17. NAME OF REFERRING PHYSICIAN OR OTHER SOURCE	17a. ___ 17b. NPI	18. HOSPITALIZATION DATES RELATED TO CURRENT SERVICES FROM MM DD YY TO MM DD YY
19. ADDITIONAL CLAIM INFORMATION (Designated by NUCC)		20. OUTSIDE LAB? ☐ YES X NO $ CHARGES

21. DIAGNOSIS OR NATURE OF ILLNESS OR INJURY. (Relate A-L, to service line below (24E))   ICD Ind. 0

A. F4323   B. ___   C. ___   D. ___
E. ___   F. ___   G. ___   H. ___
I. ___   J. ___   K. ___   L. ___

22. RESUBMISSION CODE	ORIGINAL REF. NO.
23. PRIOR AUTHORIZATION NUMBER	

24. A. DATE(S) OF SERVICE		B. PLACE OF SERVICE	C. EMG	D. PROCEDURES, SERVICES, OR SUPPLIES		E. DIAGNOSIS POINTER	F. $ CHARGES	G. DAYS OR UNITS	H. EPSDT Family Plan	I. ID. QUAL.	J. RENDERING PROVIDER ID. #
From MM DD YY	To MM DD YY			CPT/HCPCS	MODIFIER						
10 02 15	10 02 15	11	N	90846		A	150 00	1		NPI	1386713956
										NPI	
										NPI	
										NPI	
										NPI	
										NPI	

25. FEDERAL TAX I.D. NUMBER SSN EIN	26. PATIENT'S ACCOUNT NO.	27. ACCEPT ASSIGNMENT? (For govt. claims, see back)	28. TOTAL CHARGE	29. AMOUNT PAID	30. Rsvd for NUCC
123456789 X	24	X YES ☐ NO	$ 150 00	$ 0 00	

31. SIGNATURE OF PHYSICIAN OR SUPPLIER INCLUDING DEGREES OR CREDENTIALS (I certify that the statements on the reverse apply to this bill and are made a part thereof.) Roger Karam LCSW SIGNED 01 12 2016 DATE	32. SERVICE FACILITY LOCATION INFORMATION Middleville Healthcare 466 Black River Blvd Rome NY 13440 a. 1285692673 b.	33. BILLING PROVIDER INFO & PH # 315 337 3000 Middleville Healthcare 466 Black River Blvd Rome NY 13440 a. 1285692673 b.

NUCC Instruction Manual available at: www.nucc.org   PLEASE PRINT OR TYPE   APPROVED OMB-0938-1197 FORM 1500 (

1500

HEALTH INSURANCE CLAIM FORM
APPROVED BY NATIONAL UNIFORM CLAIM COMMITTEE (NUCC) 02/12

Excellus Blue Cross
P O Box 229999
Rochester NY 14692

| | PICA | | | | | | | | PICA | | |

1. MEDICARE (Medicare #)   **MEDICAID** (Medicaid #)   **TRICARE** (Sponsor's SSN)   **CHAMPVA** (Member ID#) [X]   **GROUP HEALTH PLAN** (SSN or ID)   **FECA BLK LUNG** (SSN)   **OTHER** (ID)

1a. INSURED'S I.D. NUMBER (For Program in Item 1)
ANY5555R6666

2. PATIENT'S NAME (Last Name, First Name, Middle Initial)
Franks, Marjory, M

3. PATIENT'S BIRTH DATE   **SEX**
MM 05 DD 16 YY 1948   M   F [X]

4. INSURED'S NAME (Last Name, First Name, Middle Initial)
Franks, Marjory, M

5. PATIENT'S ADDRESS (No., Street)
45 Madison St

6. PATIENT RELATIONSHIP TO INSURED
Self [X]   Spouse   Child   Other

7. INSURED'S ADDRESS (No., Street)
45 Madison St

CITY: Rome   STATE: NY

8. RESERVED FOR NUCC USE

CITY: Rome   STATE: NY

ZIP CODE: 13440   TELEPHONE (Include Area Code)

ZIP CODE: 13440   TELEPHONE (Include Area Code)

9. OTHER INSURED'S NAME (Last Name, First Name, Middle Initial)

10. IS PATIENT'S CONDITION RELATED TO:

11. INSURED'S POLICY GROUP OR FECA NUMBER

a. OTHER INSURED'S POLICY OR GROUP NUMBER

a. EMPLOYMENT? (Current or Previous)
YES   [X] NO

a. INSURED'S DATE OF BIRTH   **SEX**
MM 05 DD 16 YY 1948   M   F [X]

b. RESERVED FOR NUCC USE

b. AUTO ACCIDENT?   PLACE (State)
YES   [X] NO

b. OTHER CLAIM ID (Designated by NUCC)

c. RESERVED FOR NUCC USE

c. OTHER ACCIDENT?
YES   [X] NO

c. INSURANCE PLAN NAME OR PROGRAM NAME
Excellus Blue Cross

d. INSURANCE PLAN NAME OR PROGRAM NAME

10d. CLAIM CODES (Designated by NUCC)

d. IS THERE ANOTHER HEALTH BENEFIT PLAN?
YES   [X] NO   If yes, complete items 9, 9a, and 9d.

READ BACK OF FORM BEFORE COMPLETING & SIGNING THIS FORM
12. PATIENT'S OR AUTHORIZED PERSON'S SIGNATURE I authorize the release of any medical or other information necessary to process this claim. I also request payment of government benefits either to myself or to the party who accepts assignment below.

SIGNED: Signature on file   DATE: 01 12 2016

13. INSURED'S OR AUTHORIZED PERSON'S SIGNATURE I authorize payment of medical benefits to the undersigned physician or supplier for services described below.

SIGNED: Signature on file

14. DATE OF CURRENT ILLNESS, INJURY, or PREGNANCY (LMP)
MM DD YY   QUAL.

15. OTHER DATE   QUAL.   MM DD YY

16. DATES PATIENT UNABLE TO WORK IN CURRENT OCCUPATION
FROM MM DD YY   TO MM DD YY

17. NAME OF REFERRING PHYSICIAN OR OTHER SOURCE
17a.
17b. NPI

18. HOSPITALIZATION DATES RELATED TO CURRENT SERVICES
FROM MM DD YY   TO MM DD YY

19. ADDITIONAL CLAIM INFORMATION (Designated by NUCC)

20. OUTSIDE LAB? $ CHARGES
YES   [X] NO

21. DIAGNOSIS OR NATURE OF ILLNESS OR INJURY. (Relate A-L to service line below (24E)   ICD Ind. **0**

A. F4323   B.   C.   D.
E.   F.   G.   H.
I.   J.   K.   L.

22. RESUBMISSION CODE   ORIGINAL REF. NO.

23. PRIOR AUTHORIZATION NUMBER

24. A. DATE(S) OF SERVICE From / To			B. PLACE OF SERVICE	C. EMG	D. PROCEDURES, SERVICES, OR SUPPLIES (Explain Unusual Circumstances) CPT/HCPCS / MODIFIER	E. DIAGNOSIS POINTER	F. $ CHARGES	G. DAYS OR UNITS	H. EPSDT Family Plan	I. ID. QUAL.	J. RENDERING PROVIDER ID. #
MM DD YY	MM DD YY										
10 20 15	10 20 15		11	N	90847	A	150 00	1		NPI	1386713956
										NPI	
										NPI	
										NPI	
										NPI	
										NPI	

25. FEDERAL TAX I.D. NUMBER   SSN EIN
123456789   [X]

26. PATIENT'S ACCOUNT NO.
27

27. ACCEPT ASSIGNMENT? (For govt. claims, see back)
[X] YES   NO

28. TOTAL CHARGE
$ 150 00

29. AMOUNT PAID
$ 0 00

30. Rsvd for NUCC Use

31. SIGNATURE OF PHYSICIAN OR SUPPLIER INCLUDING DEGREES OR CREDENTIALS (I certify that the statements on the reverse apply to this bill and are made a part thereof.)
[Ro]ger Karam LCSW
DATE 01 12 2016

32. SERVICE FACILITY LOCATION INFORMATION
Middleville Healthcare
466 Black River Blvd
Rome NY 13440
a. 1285692673   b.

33. BILLING PROVIDER INFO & PH #   315 337 3000
Middleville Healthcare
466 Black River Blvd
Rome NY 13440
a. 1285692673   b.

NUCC Instruction Manual available at: www.nucc.org   PLEASE PRINT OR TYPE   APPROVED OMB-0938-1197 FORM 1500 (02-12)

1500

HEALTH INSURANCE CLAIM FORM

APPROVED BY NATIONAL UNIFORM CLAIM COMMITTEE (NUCC) 02/12

Excellus Blue Cross
P O Box 229999
Rochester NY 14692

| PICA | | | | | | | | | PICA |

1. MEDICARE	MEDICAID	TRICARE	CHAMPVA	GROUP HEALTH PLAN	FECA BLK LUNG	OTHER	1a. INSURED'S I.D. NUMBER (For Program in Item 1)
(Medicare #)	(Medicaid #)	(Sponsor's SSN)	(Member ID#) X	(SSN or ID)	(SSN)	(ID)	YAR0527B6689

2. PATIENT'S NAME (Last Name, First Name, Middle Initial)
James, William, P

3. PATIENT'S BIRTH DATE MM 04 DD 01 YY 1988 **SEX** M X F

4. INSURED'S NAME (Last Name, First Name, Middle Initial)
James, William, P

5. PATIENT'S ADDRESS (No., Street)
23 Main St

6. PATIENT RELATIONSHIP TO INSURED
Self X Spouse Child Other

7. INSURED'S ADDRESS (No., Street)
23 Main St

CITY Utica STATE NY

8. RESERVED FOR NUCC USE

CITY Utica STATE NY

ZIP CODE 13502 TELEPHONE (Include Area Code)

ZIP CODE 13502 TELEPHONE (Include Area Code)

9. OTHER INSURED'S NAME (Last Name, First Name, Middle Initial)

10. IS PATIENT'S CONDITION RELATED TO:

11. INSURED'S POLICY GROUP OR FECA NUMBER

a. OTHER INSURED'S POLICY OR GROUP NUMBER

a. EMPLOYMENT? (Current or Previous)
YES X NO

a. INSURED'S DATE OF BIRTH MM 04 DD 01 YY 1988 **SEX** M X F

b. RESERVED FOR NUCC USE

b. AUTO ACCIDENT? PLACE (State)
YES X NO

b. OTHER CLAIM ID (Designated by NUCC)

c. RESERVED FOR NUCC USE

c. OTHER ACCIDENT?
YES X NO

c. INSURANCE PLAN NAME OR PROGRAM NAME
Excellus Blue Cross

d. INSURANCE PLAN NAME OR PROGRAM NAME

10d. CLAIM CODES (Designated by NUCC)

d. IS THERE ANOTHER HEALTH BENEFIT PLAN?
YES X NO **If yes,** complete items 9, 9a, and 9d.

READ BACK OF FORM BEFORE COMPLETING & SIGNING THIS FORM

12. PATIENT'S OR AUTHORIZED PERSON'S SIGNATURE I authorize the release of any medical or other information necessary to process this claim. I also request payment of government benefits either to myself or to the party who accepts assignment below.

SIGNED Signature on file DATE 01 12 2016

13. INSURED'S OR AUTHORIZED PERSON'S SIGNATURE I authorize payment of medical benefits to the undersigned physician or supplier for services described below.

SIGNED Signature on file

14. DATE OF CURRENT ILLNESS, INJURY, or PREGNANCY (LMP) MM DD YY QUAL.

15. OTHER DATE QUAL. MM DD YY

16. DATES PATIENT UNABLE TO WORK IN CURRENT OCCUPATION FROM MM DD YY TO MM DD YY

17. NAME OF REFERRING PHYSICIAN OR OTHER SOURCE
17a.
17b. NPI

18. HOSPITALIZATION DATES RELATED TO CURRENT SERVICES FROM MM DD YY TO MM DD YY

19. ADDITIONAL CLAIM INFORMATION (Designated by NUCC)

20. OUTSIDE LAB? YES X NO $ CHARGES

21. DIAGNOSIS OR NATURE OF ILLNESS OR INJURY. (Relate A-L, to service line below (24E) ICD Ind. 0

A. F3181 B. C. D.
E. F. G. H.
I. J. K. L.

22. RESUBMISSION CODE ORIGINAL REF. NO.

23. PRIOR AUTHORIZATION NUMBER

24. A. DATE(S) OF SERVICE From MM DD YY	To MM DD YY	B. PLACE OF SERVICE	C. EMG	D. PROCEDURES, SERVICES, OR SUPPLIES (Explain Unusual Circumstances) CPT/HCPCS MODIFIER	E. DIAGNOSIS POINTER	F. $ CHARGES	G. DAYS OR UNITS	H. EPSDT Family Plan	I. ID. QUAL.	J. RENDERING PROVIDER ID. #
10 24 15	10 24 15	11	N	99213	A	125 00	1		NPI	1700813956
									NPI	
									NPI	
									NPI	
									NPI	
									NPI	

25. FEDERAL TAX I.D. NUMBER SSN EIN
123456789 X

26. PATIENT'S ACCOUNT NO.
28

27. ACCEPT ASSIGNMENT? (For govt. claims, see back)
X YES NO

28. TOTAL CHARGE $ 125 00

29. AMOUNT PAID $ 0 00

30. Rsvd for NUCC

31. SIGNATURE OF PHYSICIAN OR SUPPLIER INCLUDING DEGREES OR CREDENTIALS (I certify that the statements on the reverse apply to this bill and are made a part thereof.)
Susan Meyer DC
SIGNED DATE 01 12 2016

32. SERVICE FACILITY LOCATION INFORMATION
Middleville Healthcare
466 Black River Blvd
Rome NY 13440
a.1285692673 b.

33. BILLING PROVIDER INFO & PH # 315 337 3000
Middleville Healthcare
466 Black River Blvd
Rome NY 13440
a.1285692673 b.

NUCC Instruction Manual available at: www.nucc.org PLEASE PRINT OR TYPE APPROVED OMB-0938-1197 FORM 1500

1500

HEALTH INSURANCE CLAIM FORM

APPROVED BY NATIONAL UNIFORM CLAIM COMMITTEE (NUCC) 02/12

Excellus Blue Cross
P O Box 229999
Rochester NY 14692

PICA								PICA

MEDICARE	MEDICAID	TRICARE	CHAMPVA	GROUP HEALTH PLAN	FECA BLK LUNG	OTHER	1a. INSURED'S I.D. NUMBER (For Program in Item 1)
(Medicare #)	(Medicaid #)	(Sponsor's SSN)	(Member ID#) X	(SSN or ID)	(SSN)	(ID)	MAD5555A6666

2. PATIENT'S NAME (Last Name, First Name, Middle Initial)
Smith, Alice

3. PATIENT'S BIRTH DATE MM 05 DD 15 YY 1955 **SEX** M ☐ F X

4. INSURED'S NAME (Last Name, First Name, Middle Initial)
Smith, Alice

5. PATIENT'S ADDRESS (No., Street)
8145 Old River Rd

6. PATIENT RELATIONSHIP TO INSURED
Self X Spouse ☐ Child ☐ Other ☐

7. INSURED'S ADDRESS (No., Street)
8145 Old River Rd

CITY Holland Patent **STATE** NY

8. RESERVED FOR NUCC USE

CITY Holland Patent **STATE** NY

ZIP CODE 13354 **TELEPHONE (Include Area Code)**

ZIP CODE 13354 **TELEPHONE (Include Area Code)**

9. OTHER INSURED'S NAME (Last Name, First Name, Middle Initial)

10. IS PATIENT'S CONDITION RELATED TO:

11. INSURED'S POLICY GROUP OR FECA NUMBER

a. OTHER INSURED'S POLICY OR GROUP NUMBER

a. EMPLOYMENT? (Current or Previous) ☐ YES X NO

a. INSURED'S DATE OF BIRTH MM 05 DD 15 YY 1955 **SEX** M ☐ F X

b. RESERVED FOR NUCC USE

b. AUTO ACCIDENT? ☐ YES X NO **PLACE (State)**

b. OTHER CLAIM ID (Designated by NUCC)

c. RESERVED FOR NUCC USE

c. OTHER ACCIDENT? ☐ YES X NO

c. INSURANCE PLAN NAME OR PROGRAM NAME
Excellus Blue Cross

d. INSURANCE PLAN NAME OR PROGRAM NAME

10d. CLAIM CODES (Designated by NUCC)

d. IS THERE ANOTHER HEALTH BENEFIT PLAN?
☐ YES X NO **If yes,** complete items 9, 9a, and 9d.

READ BACK OF FORM BEFORE COMPLETING & SIGNING THIS FORM
12. PATIENT'S OR AUTHORIZED PERSON'S SIGNATURE I authorize the release of any medical or other information necessary to process this claim. I also request payment of government benefits either to myself or to the party who accepts assignment below.

SIGNED Signature on file DATE 01 12 2016

13. INSURED'S OR AUTHORIZED PERSON'S SIGNATURE I authorize payment of medical benefits to the undersigned physician or supplier for services described below.

SIGNED Signature on file

14. DATE OF CURRENT ILLNESS, INJURY, or PREGNANCY (LMP) MM DD YY QUAL.

15. OTHER DATE QUAL. MM DD YY

16. DATES PATIENT UNABLE TO WORK IN CURRENT OCCUPATION FROM MM DD YY TO MM DD YY

17. NAME OF REFERRING PHYSICIAN OR OTHER SOURCE
17a.
17b. NPI

18. HOSPITALIZATION DATES RELATED TO CURRENT SERVICES FROM MM DD YY TO MM DD YY

19. ADDITIONAL CLAIM INFORMATION (Designated by NUCC)

20. OUTSIDE LAB? ☐ YES X NO **$ CHARGES**

21. DIAGNOSIS OR NATURE OF ILLNESS OR INJURY. (Relate A-L, to service line below (24E) ICD Ind. 0
A. F4325 B. C. D.
F. G. H.
J. K. L.

22. RESUBMISSION CODE ORIGINAL REF. NO.

23. PRIOR AUTHORIZATION NUMBER

24. A. DATE(S) OF SERVICE						B. PLACE OF SERVICE	C. EMG	D. PROCEDURES, SERVICES, OR SUPPLIES		E. DIAGNOSIS POINTER	F. $ CHARGES	G. DAYS OR UNITS	H. EPSDT Family Plan	I. ID. QUAL.	J. RENDERING PROVIDER ID. #
From MM	DD	YY	To MM	DD	YY			CPT/HCPCS	MODIFIER						
10	18	15	10	18	15	11	N	90853		A	50 00	1		NPI	1700838596
														NPI	
														NPI	
														NPI	
														NPI	
														NPI	

25. FEDERAL TAX I.D. NUMBER SSN EIN
123456789 X

26. PATIENT'S ACCOUNT NO.
29

27. ACCEPT ASSIGNMENT? (For govt. claims, see back) X YES ☐ NO

28. TOTAL CHARGE $ 50 00

29. AMOUNT PAID $ 0 00

30. Rsvd for NUCC Use

31. SIGNATURE OF PHYSICIAN OR SUPPLIER INCLUDING DEGREES OR CREDENTIALS (I certify that the statements on the reverse apply to this bill and are made a part thereof.)
ul Scott DC
01 12 2016
SIGNED DATE

32. SERVICE FACILITY LOCATION INFORMATION
Middleville Healthcare
466 Black River Blvd
Rome NY 13440
a.1285692673 b.

33. BILLING PROVIDER INFO & PH # 315 337 3000
Middleville Healthcare
466 Black River Blvd
Rome NY 13440
a.1285692673 b.

NUCC Instruction Manual available at: www.nucc.org PLEASE PRINT OR TYPE APPROVED OMB-0938-1197 FORM 1500 (02-12)

1500

HEALTH INSURANCE CLAIM FORM

APPROVED BY NATIONAL UNIFORM CLAIM COMMITTEE (NUCC) 02/12

Excellus Blue Cross
P O Box 229999
Rochester NY 14692

PICA								PICA

1. MEDICARE	MEDICAID	TRICARE	CHAMPVA	GROUP HEALTH PLAN	FECA BLK LUNG	OTHER	1a. INSURED'S I.D. NUMBER (For Program in Item 1)
(Medicare #)	(Medicaid #)	(Sponsor's SSN)	(Member ID#) X	(SSN or ID)	(SSN)	(ID)	ANY55555B2323

2. PATIENT'S NAME (Last Name, First Name, Middle Initial)
Scotman, Travis, D

3. PATIENT'S BIRTH DATE   SEX
MM 06 DD 19 YY 1978   M X   F

4. INSURED'S NAME (Last Name, First Name, Middle Initial)
Scotman, Travis, D

5. PATIENT'S ADDRESS (No., Street)
P O Box 55

6. PATIENT RELATIONSHIP TO INSURED
Self X   Spouse   Child   Other

7. INSURED'S ADDRESS (No., Street)
P O Box 55

CITY Holland Patent   STATE NY

8. RESERVED FOR NUCC USE

CITY Holland Patent   STATE NY

ZIP CODE 13354   TELEPHONE (Include Area Code)

ZIP CODE 13354   TELEPHONE (Include Area Code)

9. OTHER INSURED'S NAME (Last Name, First Name, Middle Initial)

10. IS PATIENT'S CONDITION RELATED TO:

11. INSURED'S POLICY GROUP OR FECA NUMBER

a. OTHER INSURED'S POLICY OR GROUP NUMBER

a. EMPLOYMENT? (Current or Previous)   YES   X NO

a. INSURED'S DATE OF BIRTH
MM 06 DD 19 YY 1978   SEX M X   F

b. RESERVED FOR NUCC USE

b. AUTO ACCIDENT?   PLACE (State)   YES   X NO

b. OTHER CLAIM ID (Designated by NUCC)

c. RESERVED FOR NUCC USE

c. OTHER ACCIDENT?   YES   X NO

c. INSURANCE PLAN NAME OR PROGRAM NAME
Excellus Blue Cross

d. INSURANCE PLAN NAME OR PROGRAM NAME

10d. CLAIM CODES (Designated by NUCC)

d. IS THERE ANOTHER HEALTH BENEFIT PLAN?
YES   X NO   If yes, complete items 9, 9a, and 9d.

READ BACK OF FORM BEFORE COMPLETING & SIGNING THIS FORM

12. PATIENT'S OR AUTHORIZED PERSON'S SIGNATURE I authorize the release of any medical or other information necessary to process this claim. I also request payment of government benefits either to myself or to the party who accepts assignment below.
SIGNED Signature on file   DATE 01 12 2016

13. INSURED'S OR AUTHORIZED PERSON'S SIGNATURE I authorize payment of medical benefits to the undersigned physician or supplier for services described below.
SIGNED Signature on file

14. DATE OF CURRENT ILLNESS, INJURY, or PREGNANCY (LMP)
MM DD YY   QUAL.

15. OTHER DATE   QUAL.   MM DD YY

16. DATES PATIENT UNABLE TO WORK IN CURRENT OCCUPATION
FROM MM DD YY   TO MM DD YY

17. NAME OF REFERRING PHYSICIAN OR OTHER SOURCE
17a.
17b. NPI

18. HOSPITALIZATION DATES RELATED TO CURRENT SERVICES
FROM MM DD YY   TO MM DD YY

19. ADDITIONAL CLAIM INFORMATION (Designated by NUCC)

20. OUTSIDE LAB?   YES   X NO $ CHARGES

21. DIAGNOSIS OR NATURE OF ILLNESS OR INJURY. (Relate A-L, to service line below (24E)   ICD Ind. 9

A.   B.   C.   D.
E.   F.   G.   H.
I.   J.   K.   L.

22. RESUBMISSION CODE   ORIGINAL REF. NO.

23. PRIOR AUTHORIZATION NUMBER

24. A. DATE(S) OF SERVICE From MM DD YY	To MM DD YY	B. PLACE OF SERVICE	C. EMG	D. PROCEDURES, SERVICES, OR SUPPLIES (Explain Unusual Circumstances) CPT/HCPCS	MODIFIER	E. DIAGNOSIS POINTER	F. $ CHARGES	G. DAYS OR UNITS	H. EPSDT Family Plan	I. ID. QUAL.	J. RENDERING PROVIDER ID. #
09 19 15	09 19 15	11	N	90837		A	175 00	1		NPI	1386713956
										NPI	
										NPI	
										NPI	
										NPI	
										NPI	

25. FEDERAL TAX I.D. NUMBER   SSN EIN
123456789   X

26. PATIENT'S ACCOUNT NO.
30

27. ACCEPT ASSIGNMENT? (For govt. claims, see back)
X YES   NO

28. TOTAL CHARGE
$ 175 00

29. AMOUNT PAID
$ 0 00

30. Rsvd for NUCC

31. SIGNATURE OF PHYSICIAN OR SUPPLIER INCLUDING DEGREES OR CREDENTIALS (I certify that the statements on the reverse apply to this bill and are made a part thereof.)
Roger Karam LCSW
SIGNED   01 12 2016   DATE

32. SERVICE FACILITY LOCATION INFORMATION
Middleville Healthcare
466 Black River Blvd
Rome NY 13440
a. 1285692673   b.

33. BILLING PROVIDER INFO & PH #   315 337 3000
Middleville Healthcare
466 Black River Blvd
Rome NY 13440
a. 1285692673   b.

NUCC Instruction Manual available at: www.nucc.org   PLEASE PRINT OR TYPE   APPROVED OMB-0938-1197 FORM 1500

1500

HEALTH INSURANCE CLAIM FORM

APPROVED BY NATIONAL UNIFORM CLAIM COMMITTEE (NUCC) 02/12

Excellus Blue Cross
P O Box 229999
Rochester NY 14692

PICA | PICA

1. MEDICARE (Medicare #) □ **MEDICAID** (Medicaid #) □ **TRICARE** (Sponsor's SSN) □ **CHAMPVA** (Member ID#) □ **GROUP HEALTH PLAN** (SSN or ID) X **FECA BLK LUNG** (SSN) □ **OTHER** (ID) □

1a. INSURED'S I.D. NUMBER (For Program in Item 1)
ZFB0624P4578

2. PATIENT'S NAME (Last Name, First Name, Middle Initial)
Victor, Michael, R

3. PATIENT'S BIRTH DATE MM 05 DD 16 YY 1977 **SEX** M X F □

4. INSURED'S NAME (Last Name, First Name, Middle Initial)
Victor, Michael, R

5. PATIENT'S ADDRESS (No., Street)
66 Dominick St

6. PATIENT RELATIONSHIP TO INSURED
Self X Spouse □ Child □ Other □

7. INSURED'S ADDRESS (No., Street)
66 Dominick St

CITY Rome **STATE** NY

8. RESERVED FOR NUCC USE

CITY Rome **STATE** NY

ZIP CODE 13440 **TELEPHONE (Include Area Code)**

ZIP CODE 13440 **TELEPHONE (Include Area Code)**

9. OTHER INSURED'S NAME (Last Name, First Name, Middle Initial)

10. IS PATIENT'S CONDITION RELATED TO:

11. INSURED'S POLICY GROUP OR FECA NUMBER

a. OTHER INSURED'S POLICY OR GROUP NUMBER

a. EMPLOYMENT? (Current or Previous) YES □ NO X

a. INSURED'S DATE OF BIRTH MM 05 DD 16 YY 1977 **SEX** M X F □

b. RESERVED FOR NUCC USE

b. AUTO ACCIDENT? YES □ NO X **PLACE (State)**

b. OTHER CLAIM ID (Designated by NUCC)

c. RESERVED FOR NUCC USE

c. OTHER ACCIDENT? YES □ NO X

c. INSURANCE PLAN NAME OR PROGRAM NAME
Excellus Blue Cross

d. INSURANCE PLAN NAME OR PROGRAM NAME

10d. CLAIM CODES (Designated by NUCC)

d. IS THERE ANOTHER HEALTH BENEFIT PLAN? YES □ NO X **If yes, complete items 9, 9a, and 9d.**

READ BACK OF FORM BEFORE COMPLETING & SIGNING THIS FORM

12. PATIENT'S OR AUTHORIZED PERSON'S SIGNATURE I authorize the release of any medical or other information necessary to process this claim. I also request payment of government benefits either to myself or to the party who accepts assignment below.
SIGNED Signature on file DATE 01 12 2016

13. INSURED'S OR AUTHORIZED PERSON'S SIGNATURE I authorize payment of medical benefits to the undersigned physician or supplier for services described below.
SIGNED Signature on file

14. DATE OF CURRENT ILLNESS, INJURY, or PREGNANCY (LMP) MM DD YY QUAL.

15. OTHER DATE QUAL. MM DD YY

16. DATES PATIENT UNABLE TO WORK IN CURRENT OCCUPATION FROM MM DD YY TO MM DD YY

17. NAME OF REFERRING PHYSICIAN OR OTHER SOURCE 17a. 17b. NPI

18. HOSPITALIZATION DATES RELATED TO CURRENT SERVICES FROM MM DD YY TO MM DD YY

19. ADDITIONAL CLAIM INFORMATION (Designated by NUCC)

20. OUTSIDE LAB? YES □ NO X $ CHARGES

21. DIAGNOSIS OR NATURE OF ILLNESS OR INJURY. (Relate A-L to service line below (24E) ICD Ind. 0
A. F4323 B. C. D.
E. F. G. H.
I. J. K. L.

22. RESUBMISSION CODE ORIGINAL REF. NO.

23. PRIOR AUTHORIZATION NUMBER

24. A. DATE(S) OF SERVICE						B. PLACE OF SERVICE	C. EMG	D. PROCEDURES, SERVICES, OR SUPPLIES (Explain Unusual Circumstances) CPT/HCPCS	MODIFIER	E. DIAGNOSIS POINTER	F. $ CHARGES		G. DAYS OR UNITS	H. EPSDT Family Plan	I. ID. QUAL.	J. RENDERING PROVIDER ID. #
From MM	DD	YY	To MM	DD	YY											
10	16	15	10	16	15	11	N	90834		A	100	00	1		NPI	1386713956
															NPI	
															NPI	
															NPI	
															NPI	
															NPI	

25. FEDERAL TAX I.D. NUMBER 123456789 SSN □ EIN X

26. PATIENT'S ACCOUNT NO. 31

27. ACCEPT ASSIGNMENT? (For govt. claims, see back) YES X NO □

28. TOTAL CHARGE $ 100 00

29. AMOUNT PAID $ 0 00

30. Rsvd for NUCC Use

31. SIGNATURE OF PHYSICIAN OR SUPPLIER INCLUDING DEGREES OR CREDENTIALS (I certify that the statements on the reverse apply to this bill and are made a part thereof.)
ger Karam LCSW
DATE 01 12 2016

32. SERVICE FACILITY LOCATION INFORMATION
Middleville Healthcare
466 Black River Blvd
Rome NY 13440
a. 1285692673 b.

33. BILLING PROVIDER INFO & PH # 315 337 3000
Middleville Healthcare
466 Black River Blvd
Rome NY 13440
a. 1285692673 b.

NUCC Instruction Manual available at: www.nucc.org PLEASE PRINT OR TYPE APPROVED OMB-0938-1197 FORM 1500 (02-12)

1500

HEALTH INSURANCE CLAIM FORM

APPROVED BY NATIONAL UNIFORM CLAIM COMMITTEE (NUCC) 02/12

Excellus Blue Cross
P O Box 229999
Rochester NY 14692

| | PICA | | | | | | | | PICA |

1. MEDICARE (Medicare #) **MEDICAID** (Medicaid #) **TRICARE** (Sponsor's SSN) **CHAMPVA** (Member ID#) **GROUP HEALTH PLAN** X (SSN or ID) **FECA BLK LUNG** (SSN) **OTHER** (ID)

1a. INSURED'S I.D. NUMBER (For Program in Item 1)
ZFB0624P4578

2. PATIENT'S NAME (Last Name, First Name, Middle Initial)
Victor, Richard

3. PATIENT'S BIRTH DATE MM 07 DD 24 YY 1992 **SEX** M X F

4. INSURED'S NAME (Last Name, First Name, Middle Initial)
Victor, Michael, R

5. PATIENT'S ADDRESS (No., Street)
66 Dominick St

6. PATIENT RELATIONSHIP TO INSURED
Self X Spouse Child Other

7. INSURED'S ADDRESS (No., Street)
66 Dominick St

CITY Rome **STATE** NY

8. RESERVED FOR NUCC USE

CITY Rome **STATE** NY

ZIP CODE 13440 **TELEPHONE (Include Area Code)**

ZIP CODE 13440 **TELEPHONE (Include Area Code)**

9. OTHER INSURED'S NAME (Last Name, First Name, Middle Initial)

10. IS PATIENT'S CONDITION RELATED TO:

11. INSURED'S POLICY GROUP OR FECA NUMBER

a. OTHER INSURED'S POLICY OR GROUP NUMBER

a. EMPLOYMENT? (Current or Previous) YES X NO

a. INSURED'S DATE OF BIRTH MM 05 DD 16 YY 1977 **SEX** M X F

b. RESERVED FOR NUCC USE

b. AUTO ACCIDENT? YES X NO **PLACE (State)**

b. OTHER CLAIM ID (Designated by NUCC)

c. RESERVED FOR NUCC USE

c. OTHER ACCIDENT? YES X NO

c. INSURANCE PLAN NAME OR PROGRAM NAME
Excellus Blue Cross

d. INSURANCE PLAN NAME OR PROGRAM NAME

10d. CLAIM CODES (Designated by NUCC)

d. IS THERE ANOTHER HEALTH BENEFIT PLAN? YES X NO If yes, complete items 9, 9a, and 9d.

READ BACK OF FORM BEFORE COMPLETING & SIGNING THIS FORM
12. PATIENT'S OR AUTHORIZED PERSON'S SIGNATURE I authorize the release of any medical or other information necessary to process this claim. I also request payment of government benefits either to myself or to the party who accepts assignment below.

SIGNED Signature on file DATE 01 12 2016

13. INSURED'S OR AUTHORIZED PERSON'S SIGNATURE I authorize payment of medical benefits to the undersigned physician or supplier for services described below.

SIGNED Signature on file

14. DATE OF CURRENT ILLNESS, INJURY, or PREGNANCY (LMP) MM DD YY QUAL.

15. OTHER DATE QUAL. MM DD YY

16. DATES PATIENT UNABLE TO WORK IN CURRENT OCCUPATION MM DD YY FROM TO MM DD YY

17. NAME OF REFERRING PHYSICIAN OR OTHER SOURCE
17a.
17b. NPI

18. HOSPITALIZATION DATES RELATED TO CURRENT SERVICES MM DD YY FROM TO MM DD YY

19. ADDITIONAL CLAIM INFORMATION (Designated by NUCC)

20. OUTSIDE LAB? YES X NO **$ CHARGES**

21. DIAGNOSIS OR NATURE OF ILLNESS OR INJURY. (Relate A-L, to service line below (24E) ICD Ind. 0
A. F4323 B. C. D.
E. F. G. H.
I. J. K. L.

22. RESUBMISSION CODE ORIGINAL REF. NO.

23. PRIOR AUTHORIZATION NUMBER

24. A. DATE(S) OF SERVICE From MM DD YY	To MM DD YY	B. PLACE OF SERVICE	C. EMG	D. PROCEDURES, SERVICES, OR SUPPLIES (Explain Unusual Circumstances) CPT/HCPCS MODIFIER	E. DIAGNOSIS POINTER	F. $ CHARGES	G. DAYS OR UNITS	H. EPSDT Family Plan	I. ID. QUAL.	J. RENDERING PROVIDER ID. #
10 19 15	10 19 15	11	N	90832	A	80 00	1		NPI	1386713956
									NPI	
									NPI	
									NPI	
									NPI	
									NPI	

25. FEDERAL TAX I.D. NUMBER 123456789 SSN EIN X

26. PATIENT'S ACCOUNT NO. 32

27. ACCEPT ASSIGNMENT? (For govt. claims, see back) X YES NO

28. TOTAL CHARGE $ 80 00

29. AMOUNT PAID $ 0 00

30. Rsvd for NUCC

31. SIGNATURE OF PHYSICIAN OR SUPPLIER INCLUDING DEGREES OR CREDENTIALS (I certify that the statements on the reverse apply to this bill and are made a part thereof.)
Roger Karam LCSW
SIGNED 01 12 2016 DATE

32. SERVICE FACILITY LOCATION INFORMATION
Middleville Healthcare
466 Black River Blvd
Rome NY 13440
a. 1285692673 b.

33. BILLING PROVIDER INFO & PH # 315 337 3000
Middleville Healthcare
466 Black River Blvd
Rome NY 13440
a. 1285692673 b.

NUCC Instruction Manual available at: www.nucc.org   PLEASE PRINT OR TYPE   APPROVED OMB-0938-1197 FORM 1500 (

1500

HEALTH INSURANCE CLAIM FORM

APPROVED BY NATIONAL UNIFORM CLAIM COMMITTEE (NUCC) 02/12

Cigna
P O Box 7766
Chattanoga TN 45768

| | PICA | | | | | | | PICA | |

1. MEDICARE	MEDICAID	TRICARE	CHAMPVA	GROUP HEALTH PLAN	FECA BLK LUNG	OTHER	1a. INSURED'S I.D. NUMBER	(For Program in Item 1)
(Medicare #)	(Medicaid #)	(Sponsor's SSN)	(Member ID# X)	(SSN or ID)	(SSN)	(ID)	U556780045	

2. PATIENT'S NAME (Last Name, First Name, Middle Initial)
Jones, Roger, D

3. PATIENT'S BIRTH DATE   SEX
MM 06 DD 17 YY 1981   M X   F

4. INSURED'S NAME (Last Name, First Name, Middle Initial)
Jones, Roger, D

5. PATIENT'S ADDRESS (No., Street)
P O Box 7766

6. PATIENT RELATIONSHIP TO INSURED
Self X Spouse Child Other

7. INSURED'S ADDRESS (No., Street)
P O Box 7766

CITY Chattanoga   STATE TN
8. RESERVED FOR NUCC USE
CITY Chattanoga   STATE TN

ZIP CODE 45768   TELEPHONE (Include Area Code)

ZIP CODE 45768   TELEPHONE (Include Area Code)

9. OTHER INSURED'S NAME (Last Name, First Name, Middle Initial)

10. IS PATIENT'S CONDITION RELATED TO:

11. INSURED'S POLICY GROUP OR FECA NUMBER

a. OTHER INSURED'S POLICY OR GROUP NUMBER

a. EMPLOYMENT? (Current or Previous)
YES X NO

a. INSURED'S DATE OF BIRTH
MM 06 DD 17 YY 1981   SEX M X   F

b. RESERVED FOR NUCC USE

b. AUTO ACCIDENT?   PLACE (State)
YES X NO

b. OTHER CLAIM ID (Designated by NUCC)

c. RESERVED FOR NUCC USE

c. OTHER ACCIDENT?
YES X NO

c. INSURANCE PLAN NAME OR PROGRAM NAME
Cigna

d. INSURANCE PLAN NAME OR PROGRAM NAME

10d. CLAIM CODES (Designated by NUCC)

d. IS THERE ANOTHER HEALTH BENEFIT PLAN?
YES X NO If yes, complete items 9, 9a, and 9d.

READ BACK OF FORM BEFORE COMPLETING & SIGNING THIS FORM

12. PATIENT'S OR AUTHORIZED PERSON'S SIGNATURE I authorize the release of any medical or other information necessary to process this claim. I also request payment of government benefits either to myself or to the party who accepts assignment below.

SIGNED Signature on file   DATE 01 12 2016

13. INSURED'S OR AUTHORIZED PERSON'S SIGNATURE I authorize payment of medical benefits to the undersigned physician or supplier for services described below.

SIGNED Signature on file

14. DATE OF CURRENT ILLNESS, INJURY, or PREGNANCY (LMP)
MM DD YY QUAL.

15. OTHER DATE QUAL. MM DD YY

16. DATES PATIENT UNABLE TO WORK IN CURRENT OCCUPATION
FROM MM DD YY TO MM DD YY

17. NAME OF REFERRING PHYSICIAN OR OTHER SOURCE
17a.
17b. NPI

18. HOSPITALIZATION DATES RELATED TO CURRENT SERVICES
FROM MM DD YY TO MM DD YY

19. ADDITIONAL CLAIM INFORMATION (Designated by NUCC)

20. OUTSIDE LAB? $ CHARGES
YES X NO

21. DIAGNOSIS OR NATURE OF ILLNESS OR INJURY. (Relate A-L, to service line below (24E)   ICD Ind. 9

A. B. C. D.
E. F. G. H.
I. J. K. L.

22. RESUBMISSION CODE   ORIGINAL REF. NO.

23. PRIOR AUTHORIZATION NUMBER

A. DATE(S) OF SERVICE From MM DD YY	To MM DD YY	B. PLACE OF SERVICE	C. EMG	D. PROCEDURES, SERVICES, OR SUPPLIES (Explain Unusual Circumstances) CPT/HCPCS MODIFIER	E. DIAGNOSIS POINTER	F. $ CHARGES	G. DAYS OR UNITS	H. EPSDT Family Plan	I. ID. QUAL.	J. RENDERING PROVIDER ID. #
9 30 15	09 30 15	11	N	90832	A	80 00	1		NPI	1700838596
									NPI	
									NPI	
									NPI	
									NPI	
									NPI	

25. FEDERAL TAX I.D. NUMBER SSN EIN
123456789   X

26. PATIENT'S ACCOUNT NO.
25

27. ACCEPT ASSIGNMENT? (For govt. claims, see back)
X YES NO

28. TOTAL CHARGE
$ 80 00

29. AMOUNT PAID
$ 0 00

30. Rsvd for NUCC Use

31. SIGNATURE OF PHYSICIAN OR SUPPLIER INCLUDING DEGREES OR CREDENTIALS (I certify that the statements on the reverse apply to this bill and are made a part thereof.)
Paul Scott DC
01 12 2016
SIGNED DATE

32. SERVICE FACILITY LOCATION INFORMATION
Middleville Healthcare
466 Black River Blvd
Rome NY 13440
a. 1285692673 b.

33. BILLING PROVIDER INFO & PH #   315 337 3000
Middleville Healthcare
466 Black River Blvd
Rome NY 13440
a. 1285692673 b.

NUCC Instruction Manual available at: www.nucc.org   PLEASE PRINT OR TYPE   APPROVED OMB-0938-1197 FORM 1500 (02-12)

1500

HEALTH INSURANCE CLAIM FORM

APPROVED BY NATIONAL UNIFORM CLAIM COMMITTEE (NUCC) 02/12

Cigna
P O Box 7766
Chattanoga TN 45768

	PICA										PICA

1. MEDICARE (Medicare #) **MEDICAID** (Medicaid #) **TRICARE** (Sponsor's SSN) **CHAMPVA** (Member ID#) **X** **GROUP HEALTH PLAN** (SSN or ID) **FECA BLK LUNG** (SSN) **OTHER** (ID)

1a. INSURED'S I.D. NUMBER (For Program in Item 1): U54545455454

2. PATIENT'S NAME (Last Name, First Name, Middle Initial): Meyer, Raymond

3. PATIENT'S BIRTH DATE MM 01 DD 02 YY 1968   **SEX** M **X** F

4. INSURED'S NAME (Last Name, First Name, Middle Initial): Meyer, Raymond

5. PATIENT'S ADDRESS (No., Street): 103 S George St
CITY: Rome   STATE: NY
ZIP CODE: 13440   TELEPHONE (Include Area Code):

6. PATIENT RELATIONSHIP TO INSURED: Self **X** Spouse Child Other

7. INSURED'S ADDRESS (No., Street): 103 S George St
CITY: Rome   STATE: NY
ZIP CODE: 13440   TELEPHONE (Include Area Code):

8. RESERVED FOR NUCC USE

9. OTHER INSURED'S NAME (Last Name, First Name, Middle Initial)

10. IS PATIENT'S CONDITION RELATED TO:

11. INSURED'S POLICY GROUP OR FECA NUMBER

a. OTHER INSURED'S POLICY OR GROUP NUMBER

a. EMPLOYMENT? (Current or Previous) YES **X** NO

a. INSURED'S DATE OF BIRTH MM 01 DD 02 YY 1968 SEX M **X** F

b. RESERVED FOR NUCC USE

b. AUTO ACCIDENT? PLACE (State) YES **X** NO

b. OTHER CLAIM ID (Designated by NUCC)

c. RESERVED FOR NUCC USE

c. OTHER ACCIDENT? YES **X** NO

c. INSURANCE PLAN NAME OR PROGRAM NAME: Cigna

d. INSURANCE PLAN NAME OR PROGRAM NAME

10d. CLAIM CODES (Designated by NUCC)

d. IS THERE ANOTHER HEALTH BENEFIT PLAN? YES **X** NO If yes, complete items 9, 9a, and 9d.

READ BACK OF FORM BEFORE COMPLETING & SIGNING THIS FORM

12. PATIENT'S OR AUTHORIZED PERSON'S SIGNATURE I authorize the release of any medical or other information necessary to process this claim. I also request payment of government benefits either to myself or to the party who accepts assignment below.
SIGNED: Signature on file   DATE: 01 12 2016

13. INSURED'S OR AUTHORIZED PERSON'S SIGNATURE I authorize payment of medical benefits to the undersigned physician or supplier for services described below.
SIGNED: Signature on file

14. DATE OF CURRENT ILLNESS, INJURY, or PREGNANCY (LMP) MM DD YY QUAL.
15. OTHER DATE QUAL. MM DD YY
16. DATES PATIENT UNABLE TO WORK IN CURRENT OCCUPATION FROM MM DD YY TO MM DD YY

17. NAME OF REFERRING PHYSICIAN OR OTHER SOURCE 17a. 17b. NPI
18. HOSPITALIZATION DATES RELATED TO CURRENT SERVICES FROM MM DD YY TO MM DD YY

19. ADDITIONAL CLAIM INFORMATION (Designated by NUCC)
20. OUTSIDE LAB? YES **X** NO $ CHARGES

21. DIAGNOSIS OR NATURE OF ILLNESS OR INJURY. (Relate A-L, to service line below (24E)) ICD Ind. 0
A. F409 B. C. D.
E. F. G. H.
I. J. K. L.

22. RESUBMISSION CODE ORIGINAL REF. NO.
23. PRIOR AUTHORIZATION NUMBER

24. A. DATE(S) OF SERVICE From MM DD YY	To MM DD YY	B. PLACE OF SERVICE	C. EMG	D. PROCEDURES, SERVICES, OR SUPPLIES CPT/HCPCS	MODIFIER	E. DIAGNOSIS POINTER	F. $ CHARGES	G. DAYS OR UNITS	H. EPSDT Family Plan	I. ID. QUAL.	J. RENDERING PROVIDER ID. #
10 16 15	10 16 15	11	N	90853		A	50 00	1		NPI	1700838596
										NPI	
										NPI	
										NPI	
										NPI	
										NPI	

25. FEDERAL TAX I.D. NUMBER: 123456789 SSN EIN **X**
26. PATIENT'S ACCOUNT NO.: 26
27. ACCEPT ASSIGNMENT? (For govt. claims, see back) **X** YES NO
28. TOTAL CHARGE $ 50 00
29. AMOUNT PAID $ 0 00
30. Rsvd for NUCC

31. SIGNATURE OF PHYSICIAN OR SUPPLIER INCLUDING DEGREES OR CREDENTIALS (I certify that the statements on the reverse apply to this bill and are made a part thereof.)
Paul Scott DC   SIGNED   DATE 01 12 2016

32. SERVICE FACILITY LOCATION INFORMATION: Middleville Healthcare 466 Black River Blvd Rome NY 13440
a. 1285692673 b.

33. BILLING PROVIDER INFO & PH #: 315 337 3000 Middleville Healthcare 466 Black River Blvd Rome NY 13440
a. 1285692673 b.

NUCC Instruction Manual available at: www.nucc.org   PLEASE PRINT OR TYPE   APPROVED OMB-0938-1197 FORM 1500

1500

HEALTH INSURANCE CLAIM FORM

APPROVED BY NATIONAL UNIFORM CLAIM COMMITTEE (NUCC) 02/12

National Government Services
P O Box 6189
Indianapolis IN 46206

PICA								PICA

1. MEDICARE	MEDICAID	TRICARE	CHAMPVA	GROUP HEALTH PLAN	FECA BLK LUNG	OTHER	1a. INSURED'S I.D. NUMBER (For Program in Item 1)
(Medicare #)	(Medicaid #)	(Sponsor's SSN)	(Member ID#) X	(SSN or ID)	(SSN)	(ID)	095354422A

2. PATIENT'S NAME (Last Name, First Name, Middle Initial)	3. PATIENT'S BIRTH DATE	SEX	4. INSURED'S NAME (Last Name, First Name, Middle Initial)
Chapman, Jenny	MM 11 DD 29 YY 1942 M F X		Chapman, Jenny

5. PATIENT'S ADDRESS (No., Street)	6. PATIENT RELATIONSHIP TO INSURED	7. INSURED'S ADDRESS (No., Street)
8526 Maple St	Self X Spouse Child Other	8526 Maple St

CITY	STATE	8. RESERVED FOR NUCC USE	CITY	STATE
Boonville	NY		Boonville	NY

ZIP CODE	TELEPHONE (Include Area Code)		ZIP CODE	TELEPHONE (Include Area Code)
13309			13309	

9. OTHER INSURED'S NAME (Last Name, First Name, Middle Initial)	10. IS PATIENT'S CONDITION RELATED TO:	11. INSURED'S POLICY GROUP OR FECA NUMBER
		NONE

a. OTHER INSURED'S POLICY OR GROUP NUMBER	a. EMPLOYMENT? (Current or Previous)	a. INSURED'S DATE OF BIRTH	SEX
	YES X NO	MM 11 DD 29 YY 1942 M F X	

b. RESERVED FOR NUCC USE	b. AUTO ACCIDENT? PLACE (State)	b. OTHER CLAIM ID (Designated by NUCC)
	YES X NO	

c. RESERVED FOR NUCC USE	c. OTHER ACCIDENT?	c. INSURANCE PLAN NAME OR PROGRAM NAME
	YES X NO	National Government Services

d. INSURANCE PLAN NAME OR PROGRAM NAME	10d. CLAIM CODES (Designated by NUCC)	d. IS THERE ANOTHER HEALTH BENEFIT PLAN?
		YES X NO If yes, complete items 9, 9a, and 9d.

READ BACK OF FORM BEFORE COMPLETING & SIGNING THIS FORM

12. PATIENT'S OR AUTHORIZED PERSON'S SIGNATURE I authorize the release of any medical or other information necessary to process this claim. I also request payment of government benefits either to myself or to the party who accepts assignment below.

SIGNED Signature on file   DATE 01 12 2016

13. INSURED'S OR AUTHORIZED PERSON'S SIGNATURE I authorize payment of medical benefits to the undersigned physician or supplier for services described below.

SIGNED Signature on file

14. DATE OF CURRENT ILLNESS, INJURY, or PREGNANCY (LMP) MM DD YY QUAL.	15. OTHER DATE QUAL. MM DD YY	16. DATES PATIENT UNABLE TO WORK IN CURRENT OCCUPATION FROM MM DD YY TO MM DD YY
17. NAME OF REFERRING PHYSICIAN OR OTHER SOURCE	17a. 17b. NPI	18. HOSPITALIZATION DATES RELATED TO CURRENT SERVICES FROM MM DD YY TO MM DD YY
19. ADDITIONAL CLAIM INFORMATION (Designated by NUCC)		20. OUTSIDE LAB? $ CHARGES YES X NO

21. DIAGNOSIS OR NATURE OF ILLNESS OR INJURY. (Relate A-L to service line below (24E) ICD Ind. 9	22. RESUBMISSION CODE ORIGINAL REF. NO.
A. B. C. D. E. F. G. H. I. J. K. L.	23. PRIOR AUTHORIZATION NUMBER

24. A. DATE(S) OF SERVICE		B. PLACE OF SERVICE	C. EMG	D. PROCEDURES, SERVICES, OR SUPPLIES (Explain Unusual Circumstances)		E. DIAGNOSIS POINTER	F. $ CHARGES	G. DAYS OR UNITS	H. EPSDT Family Plan	I. ID. QUAL.	J. RENDERING PROVIDER ID. #
From MM DD YY	To MM DD YY			CPT/HCPCS	MODIFIER						
9 20 15	09 20 15	11	N	90792		A	225 00	1		NPI	1700813956
										NPI	
										NPI	
										NPI	
										NPI	
										NPI	

25. FEDERAL TAX I.D. NUMBER	SSN EIN	26. PATIENT'S ACCOUNT NO.	27. ACCEPT ASSIGNMENT? (For govt. claims, see back)	28. TOTAL CHARGE	29. AMOUNT PAID	30. Rsvd for NUCC Use
123456789	X	33	X YES NO	$ 225 00	$ 0 00	

31. SIGNATURE OF PHYSICIAN OR SUPPLIER INCLUDING DEGREES OR CREDENTIALS (I certify that the statements on the reverse apply to this bill and are made a part thereof.)	32. SERVICE FACILITY LOCATION INFORMATION	33. BILLING PROVIDER INFO & PH # 315 337 3000
san Meyer DC	Middleville Healthcare 466 Black River Blvd Rome NY 13440	Middleville Healthcare 466 Black River Blvd Rome NY 13440
SIGNED DATE 01 12 2016	a.1285692673 b.	a.1285692673 b.

NUCC Instruction Manual available at: www.nucc.org   PLEASE PRINT OR TYPE   APPROVED OMB-0938-1197 FORM 1500 (02-12)

1500

HEALTH INSURANCE CLAIM FORM

APPROVED BY NATIONAL UNIFORM CLAIM COMMITTEE (NUCC) 02/12

National Government Services
P O Box 6189
Indianapolis IN 46206

PICA			PICA

1. MEDICARE (Medicare #)   **MEDICAID** (Medicaid #)   **TRICARE** (Sponsor's SSN)   **CHAMPVA** (Member ID#) **X**   **GROUP HEALTH PLAN** (SSN or ID)   **FECA BLK LUNG** (SSN)   **OTHER** (ID)

1a. INSURED'S I.D. NUMBER (For Program in Item 1)
545668877B

2. PATIENT'S NAME (Last Name, First Name, Middle Initial)
Marcky, Joseph, W

3. PATIENT'S BIRTH DATE MM 07 DD 08 YY 1915   **SEX** M **X** F

4. INSURED'S NAME (Last Name, First Name, Middle Initial)
Marcky, Joseph, W

5. PATIENT'S ADDRESS (No., Street)
236 Jefferson Dr

6. PATIENT RELATIONSHIP TO INSURED
Self **X**   Spouse   Child   Other

7. INSURED'S ADDRESS (No., Street)
236 Jefferson Dr

CITY Utica   STATE NY

8. RESERVED FOR NUCC USE

CITY Utica   STATE NY

ZIP CODE 13502   TELEPHONE (Include Area Code)

ZIP CODE 13502   TELEPHONE (Include Area Code)

9. OTHER INSURED'S NAME (Last Name, First Name, Middle Initial)

10. IS PATIENT'S CONDITION RELATED TO:

11. INSURED'S POLICY GROUP OR FECA NUMBER
NONE

a. OTHER INSURED'S POLICY OR GROUP NUMBER

a. EMPLOYMENT? (Current or Previous)
YES **X** NO

a. INSURED'S DATE OF BIRTH MM 07 DD 08 YY 1915   **SEX** M **X** F

b. RESERVED FOR NUCC USE

b. AUTO ACCIDENT? PLACE (State)
YES **X** NO

b. OTHER CLAIM ID (Designated by NUCC)

c. RESERVED FOR NUCC USE

c. OTHER ACCIDENT?
YES **X** NO

c. INSURANCE PLAN NAME OR PROGRAM NAME
National Government Services

d. INSURANCE PLAN NAME OR PROGRAM NAME

10d. CLAIM CODES (Designated by NUCC)

d. IS THERE ANOTHER HEALTH BENEFIT PLAN?
YES **X** NO If yes, complete items 9, 9a, and 9d.

READ BACK OF FORM BEFORE COMPLETING & SIGNING THIS FORM

12. PATIENT'S OR AUTHORIZED PERSON'S SIGNATURE I authorize the release of any medical or other information necessary to process this claim. I also request payment of government benefits either to myself or to the party who accepts assignment below.

SIGNED Signature on file   DATE 01 12 2016

13. INSURED'S OR AUTHORIZED PERSON'S SIGNATURE I authorize payment of medical benefits to the undersigned physician or supplier for services described below.

SIGNED Signature on file

14. DATE OF CURRENT ILLNESS, INJURY, or PREGNANCY (LMP) MM DD YY QUAL.

15. OTHER DATE QUAL. MM DD YY

16. DATES PATIENT UNABLE TO WORK IN CURRENT OCCUPATION FROM MM DD YY TO MM DD YY

17. NAME OF REFERRING PHYSICIAN OR OTHER SOURCE
17a.
17b. NPI

18. HOSPITALIZATION DATES RELATED TO CURRENT SERVICES FROM MM DD YY TO MM DD YY

19. ADDITIONAL CLAIM INFORMATION (Designated by NUCC)

20. OUTSIDE LAB? YES **X** NO $ CHARGES

21. DIAGNOSIS OR NATURE OF ILLNESS OR INJURY. (Relate A-L, to service line below (24E) ICD Ind. 0

A. F4323   B.   C.   D.
E.   F.   G.   H.
I.   J.   K.   L.

22. RESUBMISSION CODE ORIGINAL REF. NO.

23. PRIOR AUTHORIZATION NUMBER

24. A. DATE(S) OF SERVICE From / To		B. PLACE OF SERVICE	C. EMG	D. PROCEDURES, SERVICES, OR SUPPLIES (Explain Unusual Circumstances) CPT/HCPCS / MODIFIER	E. DIAGNOSIS POINTER	F. $ CHARGES	G. DAYS OR UNITS	H. EPSDT Family Plan	I. ID. QUAL.	J. RENDERING PROVIDER ID. #
10 18 15	10 18 15	32	N	90846	A	150 00	1		NPI	1700838596
									NPI	
									NPI	
									NPI	
									NPI	
									NPI	

25. FEDERAL TAX I.D. NUMBER SSN EIN
123456789 **X**

26. PATIENT'S ACCOUNT NO.
34

27. ACCEPT ASSIGNMENT? (For govt. claims, see back)
X YES   NO

28. TOTAL CHARGE $ 150 00

29. AMOUNT PAID $ 0 00

30. Rsvd for NUCC

31. SIGNATURE OF PHYSICIAN OR SUPPLIER INCLUDING DEGREES OR CREDENTIALS (I certify that the statements on the reverse apply to this bill and are made a part thereof.)
Paul Scott DC
SIGNED 01 12 2016 DATE

32. SERVICE FACILITY LOCATION INFORMATION
Sunset Nursing Home
1500 Sunset St
Utica NY 13502
a.   b.

33. BILLING PROVIDER INFO & PH # 315 337 3000
Middleville Healthcare
466 Black River Blvd
Rome NY 13440
a. 1285692673   b.

NUCC Instruction Manual available at: www.nucc.org   PLEASE PRINT OR TYPE   APPROVED OMB-0938-1197 FORM 1500

1500

HEALTH INSURANCE CLAIM FORM

APPROVED BY NATIONAL UNIFORM CLAIM COMMITTEE (NUCC) 02/12

National Government Services
P O Box 6189
Indianapolis IN 46206

| PICA | | | | | | | | PICA |

1. MEDICARE	MEDICAID	TRICARE	CHAMPVA	GROUP HEALTH PLAN	FECA BLK LUNG	OTHER	1a. INSURED'S I.D. NUMBER (For Program in Item 1)
(Medicare #)	(Medicaid #)	(Sponsor's SSN)	(Member ID#) X	(SSN or ID)	(SSN)	(ID)	054889703A

2. PATIENT'S NAME (Last Name, First Name, Middle Initial)	3. PATIENT'S BIRTH DATE / SEX	4. INSURED'S NAME (Last Name, First Name, Middle Initial)
Reading, Frank, R	MM 04 DD 30 YY 1940 M X F	Reading, Frank, R

5. PATIENT'S ADDRESS (No., Street)	6. PATIENT RELATIONSHIP TO INSURED	7. INSURED'S ADDRESS (No., Street)
226 James St	Self X Spouse Child Other	226 James St

CITY	STATE	8. RESERVED FOR NUCC USE	CITY	STATE
Utica	NY		Utica	NY

ZIP CODE	TELEPHONE (Include Area Code)		ZIP CODE	TELEPHONE (Include Area Code)
13502			13502	

9. OTHER INSURED'S NAME (Last Name, First Name, Middle Initial)	10. IS PATIENT'S CONDITION RELATED TO:	11. INSURED'S POLICY GROUP OR FECA NUMBER
		NONE

a. OTHER INSURED'S POLICY OR GROUP NUMBER	a. EMPLOYMENT? (Current or Previous) YES X NO	a. INSURED'S DATE OF BIRTH MM 04 DD 30 YY 1940 SEX M X F

b. RESERVED FOR NUCC USE	b. AUTO ACCIDENT? YES X NO PLACE (State)	b. OTHER CLAIM ID (Designated by NUCC)

c. RESERVED FOR NUCC USE	c. OTHER ACCIDENT? YES X NO	c. INSURANCE PLAN NAME OR PROGRAM NAME National Government Services

d. INSURANCE PLAN NAME OR PROGRAM NAME	10d. CLAIM CODES (Designated by NUCC)	d. IS THERE ANOTHER HEALTH BENEFIT PLAN? YES X NO If yes, complete items 9, 9a, and 9d.

READ BACK OF FORM BEFORE COMPLETING & SIGNING THIS FORM

12. PATIENT'S OR AUTHORIZED PERSON'S SIGNATURE I authorize the release of any medical or other information necessary to process this claim. I also request payment of government benefits either to myself or to the party who accepts assignment below.

SIGNED Signature on file   DATE 01 12 2016

13. INSURED'S OR AUTHORIZED PERSON'S SIGNATURE I authorize payment of medical benefits to the undersigned physician or supplier for services described below.

SIGNED Signature on file

14. DATE OF CURRENT ILLNESS, INJURY, or PREGNANCY (LMP) MM DD YY QUAL.	15. OTHER DATE QUAL. MM DD YY	16. DATES PATIENT UNABLE TO WORK IN CURRENT OCCUPATION FROM MM DD YY TO MM DD YY

17. NAME OF REFERRING PHYSICIAN OR OTHER SOURCE	17a. 17b. NPI	18. HOSPITALIZATION DATES RELATED TO CURRENT SERVICES FROM MM DD YY TO MM DD YY

19. ADDITIONAL CLAIM INFORMATION (Designated by NUCC)	20. OUTSIDE LAB? YES X NO $ CHARGES

21. DIAGNOSIS OR NATURE OF ILLNESS OR INJURY. (Relate A-L, to service line below (24E) ICD Ind. 9	22. RESUBMISSION CODE ORIGINAL REF. NO.

A. B. C. D.
E. F. G. H.
I. J. K. L.

23. PRIOR AUTHORIZATION NUMBER

A. DATE(S) OF SERVICE From MM DD YY	To MM DD YY	B. PLACE OF SERVICE	C. EMG	D. PROCEDURES, SERVICES, OR SUPPLIES (Explain Unusual Circumstances) CPT/HCPCS MODIFIER	E. DIAGNOSIS POINTER	F. $ CHARGES	G. DAYS OR UNITS	H. EPSDT Family Plan	I. ID. QUAL.	J. RENDERING PROVIDER ID. #
09 20 15	09 20 15	32	N	90834	AB	100 00	1		NPI	1700838596
									NPI	
									NPI	
									NPI	
									NPI	
									NPI	

25. FEDERAL TAX I.D. NUMBER SSN EIN	26. PATIENT'S ACCOUNT NO.	27. ACCEPT ASSIGNMENT? (For govt. claims, see back)	28. TOTAL CHARGE	29. AMOUNT PAID	30. Rsvd for NUCC Use
123456789 X	35	X YES NO	$ 100 00	$ 0 00	

31. SIGNATURE OF PHYSICIAN OR SUPPLIER INCLUDING DEGREES OR CREDENTIALS (I certify that the statements on the reverse apply to this bill and are made a part thereof.) Paul Scott DC 01 12 2016 DATE	32. SERVICE FACILITY LOCATION INFORMATION Sunset Nursing Home 1500 Sunset St Utica NY 13502 a. b.	33. BILLING PROVIDER INFO & PH # 315 337 3000 Middleville Healthcare 466 Black River Blvd Rome NY 13440 a. 1285692673 b.

NUCC Instruction Manual available at: www.nucc.org   PLEASE PRINT OR TYPE   APPROVED OMB-0938-1197 FORM 1500 (02-12)

1500

HEALTH INSURANCE CLAIM FORM

APPROVED BY NATIONAL UNIFORM CLAIM COMMITTEE (NUCC) 02/12

National Government Services
P O Box 6189
Indianapolis IN 46206

PICA	PICA

1. MEDICARE (Medicare #) **MEDICAID** (Medicaid #) **TRICARE** (Sponsor's SSN) **CHAMPVA** (Member ID#) **X** **GROUP HEALTH PLAN** (SSN or ID) **FECA BLK LUNG** (SSN) **OTHER** (ID)

1a. INSURED'S I.D. NUMBER (For Program in Item 1)
022458756A

2. PATIENT'S NAME (Last Name, First Name, Middle Initial)
Riley, Betty

3. PATIENT'S BIRTH DATE MM 02 DD 13 YY 1938 **SEX** M __ F **X**

4. INSURED'S NAME (Last Name, First Name, Middle Initial)
Riley, Betty

5. PATIENT'S ADDRESS (No., Street)
5688 Thomas St

6. PATIENT RELATIONSHIP TO INSURED
Self **X** Spouse __ Child __ Other __

7. INSURED'S ADDRESS (No., Street)
5688 Thomas St

CITY Utica **STATE** NY

8. RESERVED FOR NUCC USE

CITY Utica **STATE** NY

ZIP CODE 13502 **TELEPHONE (Include Area Code)**

ZIP CODE 13502 **TELEPHONE (Include Area Code)**

9. OTHER INSURED'S NAME (Last Name, First Name, Middle Initial

10. IS PATIENT'S CONDITION RELATED TO:

11. INSURED'S POLICY GROUP OR FECA NUMBER
NONE

a. OTHER INSURED'S POLICY OR GROUP NUMBER

a. EMPLOYMENT? (Current or Previous) YES __ **X** NO

a. INSURED'S DATE OF BIRTH MM 02 DD 13 YY 1938 **SEX** M __ F **X**

b. RESERVED FOR NUCC USE

b. AUTO ACCIDENT? YES __ **X** NO PLACE (State)

b. OTHER CLAIM ID (Designated by NUCC)

c. RESERVED FOR NUCC USE

c. OTHER ACCIDENT? YES __ **X** NO

c. INSURANCE PLAN NAME OR PROGRAM NAME
National Government Services

d. INSURANCE PLAN NAME OR PROGRAM NAME

10d. CLAIM CODES (Designated by NUCC)

d. IS THERE ANOTHER HEALTH BENEFIT PLAN? YES __ **X** NO If yes, complete items 9, 9a, and 9d.

READ BACK OF FORM BEFORE COMPLETING & SIGNING THIS FORM

12. PATIENT'S OR AUTHORIZED PERSON'S SIGNATURE I authorize the release of any medical or other information necessary to process this claim. I also request payment of government benefits either to myself or to the party who accepts assignment below.
SIGNED Signature on file DATE 01 12 2016

13. INSURED'S OR AUTHORIZED PERSON'S SIGNATURE I authorize payment of medical benefits to the undersigned physician or supplier for services described below.
SIGNED Signature on file

14. DATE OF CURRENT ILLNESS, INJURY, or PREGNANCY (LMP) MM DD YY QUAL.

15. OTHER DATE QUAL. MM DD YY

16. DATES PATIENT UNABLE TO WORK IN CURRENT OCCUPATION FROM MM DD YY TO MM DD YY

17. NAME OF REFERRING PHYSICIAN OR OTHER SOURCE 17a. 17b. NPI

18. HOSPITALIZATION DATES RELATED TO CURRENT SERVICES FROM MM DD YY TO MM DD YY

19. ADDITIONAL CLAIM INFORMATION (Designated by NUCC)

20. OUTSIDE LAB? YES __ **X** NO $ CHARGES

21. DIAGNOSIS OR NATURE OF ILLNESS OR INJURY. (Relate A-L to service line below (24E) ICD Ind. **9**

A. B. C. D.
E. F. G. H.
I. J. K. L.

22. RESUBMISSION CODE ORIGINAL REF. NO.

23. PRIOR AUTHORIZATION NUMBER

24. A. DATE(S) OF SERVICE From MM DD YY	To MM DD YY	B. PLACE OF SERVICE	C. EMG	D. PROCEDURES, SERVICES, OR SUPPLIES (Explain Unusual Circumstances) CPT/HCPCS	MODIFIER	E. DIAGNOSIS POINTER	F. $ CHARGES	G. DAYS OR UNITS	H. EPSDT Family Plan	I. ID. QUAL.	J. RENDERING PROVIDER ID. #
09 20 15	09 20 15	32	N	90832		AB	80 00	1		NPI	1700838596
										NPI	
										NPI	
										NPI	
										NPI	
										NPI	

25. FEDERAL TAX I.D. NUMBER 123456789 SSN __ EIN **X**

26. PATIENT'S ACCOUNT NO. 36

27. ACCEPT ASSIGNMENT? (For govt. claims, see back) **X** YES __ NO

28. TOTAL CHARGE $ 80 00

29. AMOUNT PAID $ 0 00

30. Rsvd for NUCC

31. SIGNATURE OF PHYSICIAN OR SUPPLIER INCLUDING DEGREES OR CREDENTIALS (I certify that the statements on the reverse apply to this bill and are made a part thereof.)
Paul Scott DC
SIGNED DATE 01 12 2016

32. SERVICE FACILITY LOCATION INFORMATION
Sunset Nursing Home
1500 Sunset St
Utica NY 13502
a. b.

33. BILLING PROVIDER INFO & PH # 315 337 3000
Middleville Healthcare
466 Black River Blvd
Rome NY 13440
a. 1285692673 b.

NUCC Instruction Manual available at: www.nucc.org PLEASE PRINT OR TYPE APPROVED OMB-0938-1197 FORM 1500

1500

HEALTH INSURANCE CLAIM FORM
APPROVED BY NATIONAL UNIFORM CLAIM COMMITTEE (NUCC) 02/12

Pomco
16111
PO Box 6329
Syracuse NY 13217

| | PICA | | | | | | | | PICA | |

1. MEDICARE (Medicare #) **MEDICAID** (Medicaid #) **TRICARE** (Sponsor's SSN) **CHAMPVA** (Member ID#) X **GROUP HEALTH PLAN** (SSN or ID) **FECA BLK LUNG** (SSN) **OTHER** (ID)

1a. INSURED'S I.D. NUMBER (For Program in Item 1)
890135610

2. PATIENT'S NAME (Last Name, First Name, Middle Initial)
Andalora, Delia

3. PATIENT'S BIRTH DATE MM 06 DD 11 YY 1995 **SEX** M F X

4. INSURED'S NAME (Last Name, First Name, Middle Initial)
Andalora, Delia

5. PATIENT'S ADDRESS (No., Street)
McDonalds Road

6. PATIENT RELATIONSHIP TO INSURED
Self X Spouse Child Other

7. INSURED'S ADDRESS (No., Street)
McDonalds Road

CITY Copenhagen   STATE NY

8. RESERVED FOR NUCC USE

CITY Copenhagen   STATE NY

ZIP CODE 13626   TELEPHONE (Include Area Code)

ZIP CODE 13626   TELEPHONE (Include Area Code)

9. OTHER INSURED'S NAME (Last Name, First Name, Middle Initial

10. IS PATIENT'S CONDITION RELATED TO:

11. INSURED'S POLICY GROUP OR FECA NUMBER
910

a. OTHER INSURED'S POLICY OR GROUP NUMBER

a. EMPLOYMENT? (Current or Previous) YES X NO

a. INSURED'S DATE OF BIRTH MM 06 DD 11 YY 1995 SEX M F X

b. RESERVED FOR NUCC USE

b. AUTO ACCIDENT? PLACE (State) YES X NO

b. OTHER CLAIM ID (Designated by NUCC)

c. RESERVED FOR NUCC USE

c. OTHER ACCIDENT? YES X NO

c. INSURANCE PLAN NAME OR PROGRAM NAME
Pomco

d. INSURANCE PLAN NAME OR PROGRAM NAME

10d. CLAIM CODES (Designated by NUCC)

d. IS THERE ANOTHER HEALTH BENEFIT PLAN? YES X NO If yes, complete items 9, 9a, and 9d.

READ BACK OF FORM BEFORE COMPLETING & SIGNING THIS FORM

12. PATIENT'S OR AUTHORIZED PERSON'S SIGNATURE I authorize the release of any medical or other information necessary to process this claim. I also request payment of government benefits either to myself or to the party who accepts assignment below.

SIGNED Signature on file   DATE 01 12 2016

13. INSURED'S OR AUTHORIZED PERSON'S SIGNATURE I authorize payment of medical benefits to the undersigned physician or supplier for services described below.

SIGNED Signature on file

14. DATE OF CURRENT ILLNESS, INJURY, or PREGNANCY (LMP) MM DD YY QUAL.

15. OTHER DATE QUAL. MM DD YY

16. DATES PATIENT UNABLE TO WORK IN CURRENT OCCUPATION FROM MM DD YY TO MM DD YY

17. NAME OF REFERRING PHYSICIAN OR OTHER SOURCE

17a.
17b. NPI

18. HOSPITALIZATION DATES RELATED TO CURRENT SERVICES FROM MM DD YY TO MM DD YY

19. ADDITIONAL CLAIM INFORMATION (Designated by NUCC)

20. OUTSIDE LAB? YES X NO $ CHARGES

21. DIAGNOSIS OR NATURE OF ILLNESS OR INJURY. (Relate A-L to service line below (24E) ICD Ind. 0

A. F419 B. C. D.
E. F. G. H.
I. J. K. L.

22. RESUBMISSION CODE ORIGINAL REF. NO.

23. PRIOR AUTHORIZATION NUMBER

24. A. DATE(S) OF SERVICE From MM DD YY	To MM DD YY	B. PLACE OF SERVICE	C. EMG	D. PROCEDURES, SERVICES, OR SUPPLIES (Explain Unusual Circumstances) CPT/HCPCS	MODIFIER	E. DIAGNOSIS POINTER	F. $ CHARGES	G. DAYS OR UNITS	H. EPSDT Family Plan	I. ID. QUAL.	J. RENDERING PROVIDER ID. #
10 14 15	10 14 15	11	N	90837		A	125 00	1		NPI	1760640916
										NPI	
										NPI	
										NPI	
										NPI	
										NPI	

25. FEDERAL TAX I.D. NUMBER SSN EIN
076 62 2976 X

26. PATIENT'S ACCOUNT NO.
20

27. ACCEPT ASSIGNMENT? (For govt. claims, see back)
X YES NO

28. TOTAL CHARGE
$ 125 00

29. AMOUNT PAID
$ 0 00

30. Rsvd for NUCC Use

31. SIGNATURE OF PHYSICIAN OR SUPPLIER INCLUDING DEGREES OR CREDENTIALS (I certify that the statements on the reverse apply to this bill and are made a part thereof.)
Melanie Bush LCSW
01 12 2016
SIGNED DATE

32. SERVICE FACILITY LOCATION INFORMATION

a. b.

33. BILLING PROVIDER INFO & PH # 315 337 3000
Middleville Healthcare
466 Black River Blvd
Rome NY 13440
a.1760640916 b.

1500

HEALTH INSURANCE CLAIM FORM

APPROVED BY NATIONAL UNIFORM CLAIM COMMITTEE (NUCC) 02/12

Value Options
P O Box 1980
Latham NY 12110

| | PICA | | | | | | | | | PICA |

1. MEDICARE (Medicare #)   **MEDICAID** (Medicaid #)   **TRICARE** (Sponsor's SSN)   **CHAMPVA** (Member ID#) X   **GROUP HEALTH PLAN** (SSN or ID)   **FECA BLK LUNG** (SSN)   **OTHER** (ID)

1a. INSURED'S I.D. NUMBER (For Program in Item 1)
80055544400

2. PATIENT'S NAME (Last Name, First Name, Middle Initial)
Brown, Thomas, E

3. PATIENT'S BIRTH DATE   **SEX**
MM 12 DD 24 YY 1955   M X   F

4. INSURED'S NAME (Last Name, First Name, Middle Initial)
Brown, Thomas, E

5. PATIENT'S ADDRESS (No., Street)
123 Pretty Lane

6. PATIENT RELATIONSHIP TO INSURED
Self X   Spouse   Child   Other

7. INSURED'S ADDRESS (No., Street)
123 Pretty Lane

CITY Rome   STATE NY

8. RESERVED FOR NUCC USE

CITY Rome   STATE NY

ZIP CODE 13440   TELEPHONE (Include Area Code)

ZIP CODE 13440   TELEPHONE (Include Area Code)

9. OTHER INSURED'S NAME (Last Name, First Name, Middle Initial)

10. IS PATIENT'S CONDITION RELATED TO:

11. INSURED'S POLICY GROUP OR FECA NUMBER

a. OTHER INSURED'S POLICY OR GROUP NUMBER

a. EMPLOYMENT? (Current or Previous)   YES   X NO

a. INSURED'S DATE OF BIRTH   **SEX**
MM 12 DD 24 YY 1955   M X   F

b. RESERVED FOR NUCC USE

b. AUTO ACCIDENT?   PLACE (State)   YES   X NO

b. OTHER CLAIM ID (Designated by NUCC)

c. RESERVED FOR NUCC USE

c. OTHER ACCIDENT?   YES   X NO

c. INSURANCE PLAN NAME OR PROGRAM NAME
Value Options

d. INSURANCE PLAN NAME OR PROGRAM NAME

10d. CLAIM CODES (Designated by NUCC)

d. IS THERE ANOTHER HEALTH BENEFIT PLAN?
YES   X NO   If yes, complete items 9, 9a, and 9d.

READ BACK OF FORM BEFORE COMPLETING & SIGNING THIS FORM
12. PATIENT'S OR AUTHORIZED PERSON'S SIGNATURE I authorize the release of any medical or other information necessary to process this claim. I also request payment of government benefits either to myself or to the party who accepts assignment below.

SIGNED Signature on file   DATE 01 12 2016

13. INSURED'S OR AUTHORIZED PERSON'S SIGNATURE I authorize payment of medical benefits to the undersigned physician or supplier for services described below.

SIGNED Signature on file

14. DATE OF CURRENT ILLNESS, INJURY, or PREGNANCY (LMP) MM DD YY QUAL.

15. OTHER DATE QUAL. MM DD YY

16. DATES PATIENT UNABLE TO WORK IN CURRENT OCCUPATION MM DD YY FROM   TO MM DD YY

17. NAME OF REFERRING PHYSICIAN OR OTHER SOURCE
17a.
17b. NPI

18. HOSPITALIZATION DATES RELATED TO CURRENT SERVICES MM DD YY FROM   TO MM DD YY

19. ADDITIONAL CLAIM INFORMATION (Designated by NUCC)

20. OUTSIDE LAB? YES   X NO $ CHARGES

21. DIAGNOSIS OR NATURE OF ILLNESS OR INJURY. (Relate A-L, to service line below (24E))   ICD Ind. 0

A. F3340   B.   C.   D.
E.   F.   G.   H.
I.   J.   K.   L.

22. RESUBMISSION CODE   ORIGINAL REF. NO.

23. PRIOR AUTHORIZATION NUMBER

24. A. DATE(S) OF SERVICE						B. PLACE OF SERVICE	C. EMG	D. PROCEDURES, SERVICES, OR SUPPLIES (Explain Unusual Circumstances) CPT/HCPCS MODIFIER	E. DIAGNOSIS POINTER	F. $ CHARGES	G. DAYS OR UNITS	H. EPSDT Family Plan	I. ID. QUAL.	J. RENDERING PROVIDER ID. #
From MM	DD	YY	To MM	DD	YY									
10	17	15	10	17	15	11	N	90791	A	225 00	1		NPI	1386713956
													NPI	
													NPI	
													NPI	
													NPI	
													NPI	

25. FEDERAL TAX I.D. NUMBER   SSN EIN
123456789   X

26. PATIENT'S ACCOUNT NO.
37

27. ACCEPT ASSIGNMENT? (For govt. claims, see back)
X YES   NO

28. TOTAL CHARGE
$ 225 00

29. AMOUNT PAID
$ 0 00

30. Rsvd for NUCC

31. SIGNATURE OF PHYSICIAN OR SUPPLIER INCLUDING DEGREES OR CREDENTIALS (I certify that the statements on the reverse apply to this bill and are made a part thereof.)
Roger Karam LCSW
SIGNED   DATE 01 12 2016

32. SERVICE FACILITY LOCATION INFORMATION
Middleville Healthcare
466 Black River Blvd
Rome NY 13440
a. 1285692673   b.

33. BILLING PROVIDER INFO & PH # 315 337 3000
Middleville Healthcare
466 Black River Blvd
Rome NY 13440
a. 1285692673   b.

NUCC Instruction Manual available at: www.nucc.org   PLEASE PRINT OR TYPE   APPROVED OMB-0938-1197 FORM 1500 (

1500

HEALTH INSURANCE CLAIM FORM

APPROVED BY NATIONAL UNIFORM CLAIM COMMITTEE (NUCC) 02/12

Value Options
P O Box 1980
Latham NY 12110

| | PICA | | | | | | | PICA | |

1. MEDICARE	MEDICAID	TRICARE	CHAMPVA	GROUP HEALTH PLAN	FECA BLK LUNG	OTHER	1a. INSURED'S I.D. NUMBER (For Program in Item 1)
(Medicare #)	(Medicaid #)	(Sponsor's SSN)	(Member ID#) **X**	(SSN or ID)	(SSN)	(ID)	800456215500

2. PATIENT'S NAME (Last Name, First Name, Middle Initial)
Grems, Robert, V

3. PATIENT'S BIRTH DATE   SEX
MM 06 DD 13 YY 1951   M **X**   F

4. INSURED'S NAME (Last Name, First Name, Middle Initial)
Grems, Robert, V

5. PATIENT'S ADDRESS (No., Street)
124 Pine St

6. PATIENT RELATIONSHIP TO INSURED
Self **X** Spouse Child Other

7. INSURED'S ADDRESS (No., Street)
124 Pine St

CITY: Utica   STATE: NY

8. RESERVED FOR NUCC USE

CITY: Utica   STATE: NY

ZIP CODE: 13502   TELEPHONE (Include Area Code)

ZIP CODE: 13502   TELEPHONE (Include Area Code)

9. OTHER INSURED'S NAME (Last Name, First Name, Middle Initial)

10. IS PATIENT'S CONDITION RELATED TO:

11. INSURED'S POLICY GROUP OR FECA NUMBER

a. OTHER INSURED'S POLICY OR GROUP NUMBER

a. EMPLOYMENT? (Current or Previous)   YES **X** NO

a. INSURED'S DATE OF BIRTH
MM 06 DD 13 YY 1951   SEX M **X** F

b. RESERVED FOR NUCC USE

b. AUTO ACCIDENT?   PLACE (State)   YES **X** NO

b. OTHER CLAIM ID (Designated by NUCC)

c. RESERVED FOR NUCC USE

c. OTHER ACCIDENT?   YES **X** NO

c. INSURANCE PLAN NAME OR PROGRAM NAME
Value Options

d. INSURANCE PLAN NAME OR PROGRAM NAME

10d. CLAIM CODES (Designated by NUCC)

d. IS THERE ANOTHER HEALTH BENEFIT PLAN?
YES **X** NO   If yes, complete items 9, 9a, and 9d.

READ BACK OF FORM BEFORE COMPLETING & SIGNING THIS FORM

12. PATIENT'S OR AUTHORIZED PERSON'S SIGNATURE I authorize the release of any medical or other information necessary to process this claim. I also request payment of government benefits either to myself or to the party who accepts assignment below.

SIGNED Signature on file   DATE 01 12 2016

13. INSURED'S OR AUTHORIZED PERSON'S SIGNATURE I authorize payment of medical benefits to the undersigned physician or supplier for services described below.

SIGNED Signature on file

14. DATE OF CURRENT ILLNESS, INJURY, or PREGNANCY (LMP)
MM DD YY   QUAL.

15. OTHER DATE   QUAL.   MM DD YY

16. DATES PATIENT UNABLE TO WORK IN CURRENT OCCUPATION
FROM MM DD YY   TO MM DD YY

17. NAME OF REFERRING PHYSICIAN OR OTHER SOURCE
17a.
17b. NPI

18. HOSPITALIZATION DATES RELATED TO CURRENT SERVICES
FROM MM DD YY   TO MM DD YY

19. ADDITIONAL CLAIM INFORMATION (Designated by NUCC)

20. OUTSIDE LAB?   YES **X** NO $ CHARGES

21. DIAGNOSIS OR NATURE OF ILLNESS OR INJURY. (Relate A-L to service line below (24E)   ICD Ind. **0**

A.	B.	C.	D.
F.	G.	H.	
J.	K.	L.	

22. RESUBMISSION CODE   ORIGINAL REF. NO.

23. PRIOR AUTHORIZATION NUMBER

A. DATE(S) OF SERVICE From MM DD YY	To MM DD YY	B. PLACE OF SERVICE	C. EMG	D. PROCEDURES, SERVICES, OR SUPPLIES (Explain Unusual Circumstances) CPT/HCPCS MODIFIER	E. DIAGNOSIS POINTER	F. $ CHARGES	G. DAYS OR UNITS	H. EPSDT Family Plan	I. ID. QUAL.	J. RENDERING PROVIDER ID. #
09 17 15	09 17 15	11	N	90834	A	100 00	1		NPI	1386713956
10 15 15	10 15 15	11	N	90834	A	100 00	1		NPI	1386713956
									NPI	
									NPI	
									NPI	
									NPI	

25. FEDERAL TAX I.D. NUMBER   SSN EIN
123456789   **X**

26. PATIENT'S ACCOUNT NO.
38

27. ACCEPT ASSIGNMENT? (For govt. claims, see back)
X YES   NO

28. TOTAL CHARGE
$ 200 00

29. AMOUNT PAID
$ 0 00

30. Rsvd for NUCC Use

31. SIGNATURE OF PHYSICIAN OR SUPPLIER INCLUDING DEGREES OR CREDENTIALS (I certify that the statements on the reverse apply to this bill and are made a part thereof.)
ger Karam LCSW
01 12 2016   DATE

32. SERVICE FACILITY LOCATION INFORMATION
Middleville Healthcare
466 Black River Blvd
Rome NY 13440
a. 1285692673   b.

33. BILLING PROVIDER INFO & PH #   315 337 3000
Middleville Healthcare
466 Black River Blvd
Rome NY 13440
a. 1285692673   b.

NUCC Instruction Manual available at: www.nucc.org   PLEASE PRINT OR TYPE   APPROVED OMB-0938-1197 FORM 1500 (02-12)

1500

HEALTH INSURANCE CLAIM FORM

APPROVED BY NATIONAL UNIFORM CLAIM COMMITTEE (NUCC) 02/12

Value Options
P O Box 1980
Latham NY 12110

					PICA

1. MEDICARE	MEDICAID	TRICARE	CHAMPVA	GROUP HEALTH PLAN	FECA BLK LUNG	OTHER	1a. INSURED'S I.D. NUMBER (For Program in Item 1)
(Medicare #)	(Medicaid #)	(Sponsor's SSN)	(Member ID#) X	(SSN or ID)	(SSN)	(ID)	80054432100

2. PATIENT'S NAME (Last Name, First Name, Middle Initial)
Mack, Sally , R

3. PATIENT'S BIRTH DATE MM 04 DD 10 YY 1984 **SEX** M F X

4. INSURED'S NAME (Last Name, First Name, Middle Initial)
Mack, Sally , R

5. PATIENT'S ADDRESS (No., Street)
8054 Rt 233

6. PATIENT RELATIONSHIP TO INSURED
Self X Spouse Child Other

7. INSURED'S ADDRESS (No., Street)
8054 Rt 233

CITY Rome STATE NY

8. RESERVED FOR NUCC USE

CITY Rome STATE NY

ZIP CODE 13440 TELEPHONE (Include Area Code)

ZIP CODE 13440 TELEPHONE (Include Area Code)

9. OTHER INSURED'S NAME (Last Name, First Name, Middle Initial)

10. IS PATIENT'S CONDITION RELATED TO:

11. INSURED'S POLICY GROUP OR FECA NUMBER

a. OTHER INSURED'S POLICY OR GROUP NUMBER

a. EMPLOYMENT? (Current or Previous) YES X NO

a. INSURED'S DATE OF BIRTH MM 04 DD 10 YY 1984 SEX M F X

b. RESERVED FOR NUCC USE

b. AUTO ACCIDENT? PLACE (State) YES X NO

b. OTHER CLAIM ID (Designated by NUCC)

c. RESERVED FOR NUCC USE

c. OTHER ACCIDENT? YES X NO

c. INSURANCE PLAN NAME OR PROGRAM NAME
Value Options

d. INSURANCE PLAN NAME OR PROGRAM NAME

10d. CLAIM CODES (Designated by NUCC)

d. IS THERE ANOTHER HEALTH BENEFIT PLAN?
YES X NO If yes, complete items 9, 9a, and 9d.

READ BACK OF FORM BEFORE COMPLETING & SIGNING THIS FORM

12. PATIENT'S OR AUTHORIZED PERSON'S SIGNATURE I authorize the release of any medical or other information necessary to process this claim. I also request payment of government benefits either to myself or to the party who accepts assignment below.

SIGNED Signature on file DATE 01 12 2016

13. INSURED'S OR AUTHORIZED PERSON'S SIGNATURE I authorize payment of medical benefits to the undersigned physician or supplier for services described below.

SIGNED Signature on file

14. DATE OF CURRENT ILLNESS, INJURY, or PREGNANCY (LMP) MM DD YY QUAL.	15. OTHER DATE QUAL. MM DD YY	16. DATES PATIENT UNABLE TO WORK IN CURRENT OCCUPATION FROM MM DD YY TO MM DD YY

17. NAME OF REFERRING PHYSICIAN OR OTHER SOURCE	17a.	18. HOSPITALIZATION DATES RELATED TO CURRENT SERVICES FROM MM DD YY TO MM DD YY
	17b. NPI	

19. ADDITIONAL CLAIM INFORMATION (Designated by NUCC)

20. OUTSIDE LAB? YES X NO $ CHARGES

21. DIAGNOSIS OR NATURE OF ILLNESS OR INJURY. (Relate A-L, to service line below (24E) ICD Ind. 9

A. B. C. D.
E. F. G. H.
I. J. K. L.

22. RESUBMISSION CODE ORIGINAL REF. NO.

23. PRIOR AUTHORIZATION NUMBER

24. A. DATE(S) OF SERVICE		B. PLACE OF SERVICE	C. EMG	D. PROCEDURES, SERVICES, OR SUPPLIES (Explain Unusual Circumstances)		E. DIAGNOSIS POINTER	F. $ CHARGES	G. DAYS OR UNITS	H. EPSDT Family Plan	I. ID. QUAL.	J. RENDERING PROVIDER ID. #
From MM DD YY	To MM DD YY			CPT/HCPCS	MODIFIER						
08 19 15	08 19 15	11	N	90837		AB	175 00	1		NPI	1700838596
										NPI	
										NPI	
										NPI	
										NPI	
										NPI	

25. FEDERAL TAX I.D. NUMBER SSN EIN	26. PATIENT'S ACCOUNT NO.	27. ACCEPT ASSIGNMENT? (For govt. claims, see back)	28. TOTAL CHARGE	29. AMOUNT PAID	30. Rsvd for NUCC
123456789 X	39	X YES NO	$ 175 00	$ 0 00	

31. SIGNATURE OF PHYSICIAN OR SUPPLIER INCLUDING DEGREES OR CREDENTIALS (I certify that the statements on the reverse apply to this bill and are made a part thereof.)
Paul Scott DC
SIGNED 01 12 2016 DATE

32. SERVICE FACILITY LOCATION INFORMATION
Middleville Healthcare
466 Black River Blvd
Rome NY 13440
a. 1285692673 b.

33. BILLING PROVIDER INFO & PH # 315 337 3000
Middleville Healthcare
466 Black River Blvd
Rome NY 13440
a. 1285692673 b.

NUCC Instruction Manual available at: www.nucc.org   PLEASE PRINT OR TYPE   APPROVED OMB-0938-1197 FORM 1500

Answer Key

Claim 1:   Benjamin Clark   Aetna, indemnity plan w/ no pre-auth required – initial visit with psychologist

Claim 2:   Mary Jeffries   Aetna, indemnity plan w/ no pre-auth required - individual therapy with social worker 45-50 minutes

Claim 3:   Sally Jeffries   Aetna, indemnity plan w/ no pre-auth required - individual therapy with social worker 45-50 minutes

Claim 4:   Travis Jeffries   Aetna, indemnity plan w/ no pre-auth required - family therapy without the patient present with social worker

Claim 5:   Marjorie Franks   Blue Cross claim w/Aetna 2ndary, family therapy patient present

Claim 6:   William James   Blue Cross claim, medication management – 2 visits with Psychiartist

Claim 7:   Alice Smith   Blue Cross claim, group therapy with psychologist

Claim 8:   Travis Scotman   Blue Cross claim, indemnity plan – no pre auth required – individual therapy with social worker 75-80 minutes

Claim 9:   Michael Victor   Blue Cross claim, indemnity plan no pre-auth required – individual therapy with social worker – 45-50 minutes

Claim 10:   Richard Victor   Blue Cross claim, indemnity plan no pre-auth required – individual therapy 20-30 minutes

Claim 11:   Roger Jones   Cigna claim, individual therapy with psychologist for 2 visits – one 20-30 minutes – one 45-50 min.

Claim 12:   Raymond Meyer   Cigna claim, group therapy with psychologist – no pre-auth

Claim 13:   Jennie Chapman   Medicare claim w/BC 2ndary, initial visit with psychiatrist

Claim 14:   Joseph Marcky   Medicare claim for a nursing home patient – family therapy with a Psychologist without the patient present

Claim 15:   Frank Reading   Medicare claim for a nursing home patient with a
Psychologist for individual therapy 45-50 minutes

Claim 16:   Betty Reilly   Medicare claim for a nursing home patient with a
Psychologist for individual therapy 20-30 minutes

Claim 17:   Thomas Brown   HMO claim, initial visit with social worker

Claim 18:   Robert Brown   HMO claim, family therapy w/pt present

Claim 19:   Robert Grems   HMO claim, individual therapy with Psychologist 2
                                    Sessions 45-50 minutes

Claim 20:   Sally Mack   HMO claim, individual therapy 75-80 minutes with
social worker

Note: Some insurance carriers still use legacy numbers which are indicated in box
24J in the shaded area. Medicare will deny any claims if the provider's PTAN (or legacy
number) is in box 24J or box 33B. You will note that we do not have Medicare PTAN's
on these sample claims for that reason.

Other books available by Alice Scott and Michele Redmond – available at our website
http://www.medicalbillinglive.com

"Basics of Medical Billing" - Instantly Improve the efficiency and cash flow of your office using this guide! It's a must read for everyone from the receptionist to the doctor in any medical office!

"How to Start Your Own *Successful* Medical Billing Business" – written in 1999, revised in 2002 and again in 2007 and again in 2009. For anyone interested in starting a medical billing business, this book is a **must!**

"12 Marketing Strategies to Grow Your Medical Billing Business" – written in 2002 and revised in 2007. If you've started your medical billing service and need to find more clients, you **need** this book.

"Take Your Medical Billing Business To The Next Level" – Are you ready to expand your medical billing business? Are you ready to take on more business or hire an employee? Here are the secrets we've learned in the last 17 years from starting our own medical billing business to currently billing for over fifty providers.

"Secrets to Signing Up Your First Doctor" – Learn the secrets to finding and signing up your first accounts.

"How to Complete a UB04 Form Completely and Correctly" – Complete instructions on completing a UB04 form correctly so your claims will be paid on the first submission.

"How To Complete a CMS 1500 Completely and Correctly - Line By Line, Box By Box" Complete instructions on completing a CMS 1500 form correctly in easy to understand language.

"Chiropractic Billing Made Easy" – How to make sure your claims are paid properly and you are reimbursed completely for your chiropractic services.

"Medicare Enrollment – Completing the 855I" Instructions for completing the individual enrollment application for Medicare along with much information about how the Medicare system works.

"Write a Kick Butt Contract for Your Medical Billing Service"– East to follow instructions that walk you step by step through the process of writing a contract for your medical billing service, even if you have no idea where to start! We show you what you need to consider when writing a contract, scenarios of situations that can arise as well as sample wording to use while saving you a ton of money in lawyer's fees!

"Pricing Your Medical Billing Service" - Guide to the commonly used methods of charging for your services with the pros and cons. Make sure you are not breaking the law with one commonly used method. This book breaks down all the services you may wish to charge for.

"Denials, Appeals & Adjustments" – Guide to dealing with a variety of denials of medical insurance claims. Includes the difference between adjustments to claims and appeals. Complete guide to getting claims paid correctly.

Made in the USA
Coppell, TX
05 March 2023

13808087R00070